JEAN BAUDRILLARD

A controversial figure in the realms of theory and cultural studies, Jean Baudrillard is never without interest. But how do we make sense of his wilder statements about the postmodern world he claims we all inhabit? How do we situate his writing in relation to French thought? This book guides the reader through Baudrillard's work, from his first publication to his later postmodern statements.

Richard J. Lane offers an impressively clear introduction to key aspects of Baudrillard's thought, from his reworking of Marxism through to his theories on technology, primitivism, simulation and the hyperreal, America and the postmodern. Throughout the volume, ideas are considered in relation to the social and intellectual contexts in which Baudrillard worked, and special attention is paid to the ongoing narratives of French and postmodern thought. An extensively annotated bibliography of primary and secondary texts prepares the student reader for further encounters with Baudrillard's work.

Tracing a sure path through often complex writings, *Jean Baudrillard* is the perfect companion for those newly approaching this key contemporary thinker.

Richard J. L   ama and literature at S   d widely in these areas,   re. He is also co-direct   Studies.

D0322863

ROUTLEDGE CRITICAL THINKERS

Series Editor: Robert Eaglestone, Royal Holloway, University of London

Routledge Critical Thinkers is a series of accessible introductions to key figures in contemporary critical thought.

With a unique focus on historical and intellectual contexts, each volume examines a key theorist's:

- significance
- motivation
- key ideas and their sources
- impact on other thinkers

Concluding with extensively annotated guides to further reading, Routledge Critical Thinkers are the student's passport to today's most exciting critical thought.

For further details on this series, see *www.literature.routledge.com/rct*

JEAN BAUDRILLARD

Richard J. Lane

 Routledge
Taylor & Francis Group

LONDON AND NEW YORK

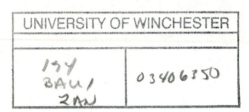
First published 2000
by Routledge
2 Park Square, Milton Park, Abingdon, Oxon, OX14 4RN

Simultaneously published in the USA and Canada
by Routledge
270 Madison Ave, New York, NY 10016

Reprinted 2001, 2004, 2006

Routledge is an imprint of the Taylor & Francis Group, an informa business

© 2000 Richard J. Lane

Typeset in Perpetua by Taylor & Francis Books Ltd
Printed and bound in Great Britain by TJ International Ltd, Padstow, Cornwall

British Library Cataloguing in Publication Data
A catalogue record for this book is available from the British Library

Library of Congress Cataloging in Publication Data
Lane, Richard J.
  Jean Baudrillard/Richard J. Lane.
    p. cm. – (Routledge critical thinkers)
  Includes bibliographical references and index.
  I. Baudrillard, Jean. I. Title. II. Series.

B2430.B33974 L36 2000
194–dc21   00-031140

ISBN 10: 0–415–21514–5 (hbk)
ISBN 10: 0–415–21515–3 (pbk)

ISBN 13: 978–0–415–21514–5 (hbk)
ISBN 13: 978–0–415–21515–3 (pbk)

CONTENTS

SERIES EDITOR'S PREFACE

The books in this series offer introductions to major critical thinkers who have influenced literary studies and the humanities. The *Routledge Critical Thinkers* series provides the books you can turn to first when a new name or concept appears in your studies.

Each book will equip you to approach a key thinker's original texts by explaining her or his key ideas, putting them into context and, perhaps most importantly, showing you why this thinker is considered to be significant. The emphasis is on concise, clearly written guides which do not presuppose a specialist knowledge. Although the focus is on particular figures, the series stresses that no critical thinker ever existed in a vacuum but, instead, emerged from a broader intellectual, cultural and social history. Finally, these books will act as a bridge between you and the thinker's original texts: not replacing them but rather complementing what she or he wrote.

These books are necessary for a number of reasons. In his 1997 autobiography, *Not Entitled*, the literary critic Frank Kermode wrote of a time in the 1960s:

> On beautiful summer lawns, young people lay together all night, recovering from their daytime exertions and listening to a troupe of Balinese musicians. Under their blankets or their sleeping bags, they would chat drowsily about the gurus of the time... What they repeated was largely hearsay; hence my lunchtime suggestion, quite impromptu, for a series of short, very cheap books offering authoritative but intelligible introductions to such figures.

There is still a need for "authoritative and intelligible introductions". But this series reflects a different world from the 1960s. New thinkers have emerged and the reputations of others have risen and fallen, as new research has developed. New methodologies and challenging ideas have spread through the arts and humanities. The study of literature is no longer – if it ever was – simply the study and evaluation of poems, novels and plays. It is also the study of the ideas, issues, and difficulties which arise in any literary text and in its interpretation. Other arts and humanities subjects have changed in analogous ways.

With these changes, new problems have emerged. The ideas and issues behind these radical changes in the humanities are often presented without reference to wider contexts or as theories which you can simply "add on" to the texts you read. Certainly, there's nothing wrong with picking out selected ideas or using what comes to hand – indeed, some thinkers have argued that this is, in fact, all we can do. However, it is sometimes forgotten that each new idea comes from the pattern and development of somebody's thought and it is important to study the range and context of their ideas. Against theories "floating in space", the *Routledge Critical Thinkers* series places key thinkers and their ideas firmly back in their contexts.

More than this, these books reflect the need to go back to the thinker's own texts and ideas. Every interpretation of an idea, even the most seemingly innocent one, offers its own "spin", implicitly or explicitly. To read only books on a thinker, rather than texts by that thinker, is to deny yourself a chance of making up your own mind. Sometimes what makes a significant figure's work hard to approach is not so much its style or content as the feeling of not knowing where to start. The purpose of these books is to give you a "way in" by offering an accessible overview of these thinkers' ideas and works and by guiding your further reading, starting with each thinker's own texts. To use a metaphor from the philosopher Ludwig Wittgenstein (1889–1951), these books are ladders, to be thrown away after you have climbed to the next level. Not only, then, do they equip you to approach new ideas, but also they empower you, by leading you back to a theorist's own texts and encouraging you to develop your own informed opinions.

Finally, these books are necessary because, just as intellectual needs have changed, the education systems around the world – the contexts in which introductory books are usually read – have changed radically, too. What was suitable for the minority higher education system of the 1960s is not suitable for the larger, wider, more diverse, high technology education systems of the twenty-first century. These changes call not just for new, up-to-date, introductions but new methods of presentation. The presentational aspects of *Routledge Critical Thinkers* have been developed with today's students in mind.

Each book in the series has a similar structure. They begin with a section offering an overview of the life and ideas of each thinker and explain why she or he is important. The central section of each book discusses the thinker's key ideas, their context, evolution and reception. Each book concludes with a survey of the thinker's impact, outlining how their ideas have been taken up and developed by others. In addition, there is a detailed final section suggesting and describing books for further reading. This is not a "tacked-on" section but an integral part of each volume. In the first part of this section you will find brief descriptions of the thinker's key works: following this, information on the most useful critical works and, in some cases, on relevant websites. This section will guide you in your reading, enabling you to follow your interests and develop your own projects. Throughout each book, references are given in what is known as the Harvard system (the author and the date of works cited are given in the text and you can look up the full details in the bibliography at the back). This offers a lot of information in very little space. The books also explain technical terms and use boxes to describe events or ideas in more detail, away from the main emphasis of the discussion. Boxes are also used at times to highlight definitions of terms frequently used or coined by a thinker. In this way, the boxes serve as a kind of glossary, easily identified when flicking through the book.

The thinkers in the series are "critical" for three reasons. First, they are examined in the light of subjects which involve criticism: principally literary studies or English and cultural studies, but also other disciplines which rely on the criticism of books, ideas, theories and unquestioned assumptions. Second, they are critical because studying their work will provide you with a "tool kit" for your own informed critical reading and thought, which will make you critical. Third, these thinkers are critical because they are crucially important: they deal with ideas and questions which can overturn conventional understandings of the world, of texts, of everything we take for granted, leaving us with a deeper understanding of what we already knew and with new ideas.

No introduction can tell you everything. However, by offering a way into critical thinking, this series hopes to begin to engage you in an activity which is productive, constructive and potentially life-changing.

WHY BAUDRILLARD?

Jean Baudrillard is not only one of the most famous writers on the subject of postmodernism, but he somehow seems to embody post-modernism itself. He is a writer and speaker whose texts are performances, attracting huge readerships or audiences. At the same time, his work is highly contentious, attracting a great deal of vitriolic criticism. He has been accused, for example, of being a critical terrorist, a nihilist (someone who has no beliefs at all, or values nothing), and a critic whose ideas are shallow and inaccurate. And yet, even given all of these harsh comments, he also has a wide critical following, with many books and articles being produced about him or using his theories to this very day. Throughout the 1990s many of Baudrillard's early works, all of which were originally written in French, were translated and made available to the English-speaking world. Thus we now have easy access to virtually all of Baudrillard's most important books, and this is leading to some reassessment of his worth as a more "serious" thinker and writer.

Baudrillard was born in Reims on the 27 July 1929. He had a fairly conventional upbringing and education. In 1956 he began teaching Sociology in secondary education, which he continued until 1966, the year he defended his thesis on *Le Système des objets* (*The System of Objects*) at the University of Paris X-Nanterre. Baudrillard's initial work was mainly known in the French-speaking world, especially his more literary articles and reviews. But after 1968, with the publication of his thesis, his writings began to become known to academics in the English-speaking world who followed developments in French theory. In 1975, Baudrillard began teaching abroad, at the University of California (Levin, 1996: xi). Baudrillard's real fame would arise not from his early fairly academic writings, but in the 1970s and 1980s with the publication of short, highly provocative critical books, published in English in the New York Semiotext(e) "Foreign Agent Series". Probably the most widely read were *Simulations* (1981) and *In the Shadow of the Silent Majorities: or, The End of the Social* (1978), both published by Semiotext(e) in 1983. Now the Western world was bombarded by Baudrillardian phrases such as "simulation", "simulacra", the "hyperreal" and the "implosion of meaning". Baudrillard was clearly a force to be reckoned with, but also someone increasingly hard to pin down as his work became more and more playful, evasive and provocative. During the 1980s and 1990s, Baudrillard travelled and lectured around the world, putting most of his energies into the "non-academic" side of his work. His travels are recorded playfully in the texts *America* and *Cool Memories*, while more "scandalous" material followed with his collection of essays published as *The Gulf War Did Not Take Place*. Baudrillard is still writing, still producing postmodern performances and texts, with more work forthcoming or available to read now in electronic format on the Internet.

INFLUENCES

When Baudrillard was a teenager, he would have experienced with the rest of the country the launch of the Monnet Plan with the slogan "modernization or downfall" (Ardagh, 1978: 32). This plan was the French government's scheme for nationwide modernization, conceived of by Jean Monnet, political economist and "father" of the EU, and focused on the rebuilding of basic industries as a way of providing stability and then growth in the economy after World War II. Successive Plans incorporated agriculture (*Second Plan*, 1953–1957), and then wider social structures such as welfare, housing and regional development (*Third Plan*, 1958–1961; *Fourth Plan*, 1962–1965) (Ardagh, 1978: 46). The Plans were designed to map out future possibilities in the country, rather than become enshrined in law; in other words, businesses were encouraged rather than forced to base their forecasting and planning upon Monnet's policies. Once each plan was launched, it was up to "reality" to fall into place. This division between official and indicative government policy, or political and structural change, would have implications for Baudrillard's writing from his thesis onwards, as we will briefly refer to in relation to theories of structuralism in Chapter 1.

Baudrillard first started to publish work in Jean-Paul Sartre's journal, *Les Temps modernes*. Sartre (1905–1980) was one of the most influential philosophers of postwar France, coordinating the movement known as *Existentialism*, essentially a philosophy thinking through the implications of life governed by human choice rather than religious order or determinism (that choices have already been made for us). While Sartre was an important influence upon a whole generation of French thinkers in general for his reading of Marxism (see p. 10), Baudrillard was also personally interested in, and teaching, German sociology and literature. The latter enabled Baudrillard to start thinking of a re-reading of Marxism that would not be heavily influenced by the "authorized" Marxism of Sartre.

In an interview with critics Mike Gane and Monique Arnaud, Baudrillard comments that he knows German culture thoroughly (Gane, 1993: 21). He uses the phrase "culture", rather than being more specific with "literature" or "philosophy", because he wants to indicate his position as a theorist on the margins of mainstream French intellectual thought; rather than having a traditional, systematic, philosophical training (like one of his key intellectual rivals, Michel Foucault [1926–1984]), Baudrillard took a far more circuitous route to success. Nonetheless, Baudrillard learnt German to read and translate some of the key texts, such as the German romantics and the philosophers Arthur Schopenhauer (1788–1860), Friedrich Nietzsche (1844–1900) and Martin Heidegger (1889–1976) (see Gane, 1993: 21). Baudrillard's marginal institutional existence is paralleled by his later publications that play at the margins of mainstream thought.

During the 1960s, Baudrillard translated, among other things, works by the playwrights Peter Weiss (1916–1982) and Bertolt Brecht (1898–1956). The influence of Weiss is usually played down; in fact, Baudrillard translated four important works: *Pointe du Fuite* (1964), *Marat/Sade* (1965), *L'Instruction* (1966) and *Discours sur la genèse et le déroulement de la très longue guerre de libération du Vietnam* (1968). Each of these texts combine cutting political statements with an undermining of stable points of view; we can think of them as precursors for Baudrillard's own approach to writing about the world. *Marat / Sade* is a play constructed according to historical facts: the murder of the French revolutionary leader Jean Paul Marat (1743–1793). Yet Weiss gives all this a complicated twist, because his play is about a performance of this murder in the Asylum of Charenton, "directed" by the Marquis de Sade (1740–1814), who *was* once imprisoned in Charenton. *Marat / Sade* becomes a play located in the historical real, but also one that dislocates history. Robert Cohen, critic and editor of Weiss' works in The German Library series, argues that such " ... a complex and disorienting structure tends to subvert attempts at assigning *Marat / Sade* a stable meaning and gives it the characteristics of a precursor of a postmodern drama of playful arbitrariness and undecidability" (1998: xiii–xiv). With Weiss' *Marat / Sade*, we have a new and interesting form for the exploration of political ideas, one which strays far from the typical Marxism that informed Weiss' thinking at the time of the play's development and production. Similarly, Baudrillard was exploring different ways of performing Marxist analyses, and we can tie in his work translating this play of "grotesque violence and sexual excess" (Cohen, 1998: xiv) with his interest in the French thinker Georges Bataille (1897–1962).

Georges Bataille during the late 1920s and 1930s constructed a theory of writing based upon the "excessive" what he called "heterogeneous matter"– that is to say, waste, excrement, excess, the illogical and the unreasonable. In other words, he focused upon those areas of society which grand philosophies ignore as part of their attempt to rise above the everyday world. Initially Bataille's work was rejected by the dominant French thinkers of the time, but he was "rediscovered" by a later wave of theorists from the 1960s onwards (Butler, 1999: 4). To understand Bataille, and the new interest in his work, is to understand the way in which modern French thinkers reacted to the constraints of Hegel and Marx (see Chapters 1 and 4); in other words, we can situate a whole host of thinkers that include Baudrillard in one stretch of narrative.

THIS BOOK

The Key Ideas section of this book will begin by examining Baudrillard's emergence from this stretch of narrative. The first chapter will examine the way in which Bataille's work was not only useful for French thinkers trying to escape from the dominance of the "grand" theories and philosophies in France at the time, but also how Baudrillard used the energies generated by these intellectual debates to fuel his own ways of thinking. The following chapters examine the ideas for which Baudrillard is best known, placing them overall in order of their development. Baudrillard's thesis text is examined to measure the importance that new technologies will have throughout his work; then the extensive references to "primitive" societies are explored, followed by a brief examination of the role of Marxism in his early writing. Three chapters on postmodernism follow, examining concepts such as the hyperreal, which have become part of the common currency of the postmodern scene. While the book progressively develops an under-standing of Baudrillard's work, readers may wish to jump straight into a particular chapter to help explain a particularly demanding or prob-lematic Baudrillardian text or idea. The Key Ideas section is followed by "After Baudrillard", a short section examining the importance and impact of Baudrillard's work for contemporary critical/cultural theo-rists. Reference is made to the ways in which Baudrillard and new technologies such as the Internet are of interest. This book seeks not to replace Baudrillard's own work by "telling readers what he says", but to provide a bridge to his rich and often challenging texts. For this reason, the book ends with a "Further Reading" section, which begins by listing Baudrillard's works and providing some information on each. A few helpful secondary texts are also listed, but the emphasis is upon how useful these texts are in accompanying study of the primary works.

KEY IDEAS

1

BEGINNINGS

French thought in the 1960s

In 1968 Jean Baudrillard published his first book with Éditions Gallimard, called *Le Système des objets*. The date of publication happens to be one of the most infamous years in recent French history, with students and workers rising up in political protest on a grand scale. Yet, it is no surprise that Baudrillard's book should coincide with such a date, because he is a thinker and writer who emerges from, and forms part of, several significant strands in contemporary French culture and theory. This chapter will examine in some detail the complicated network of philosophical influences upon Baudrillard's work, describing the background of the man who emerges from an intellectually and politically exciting (as well as demanding) period.

INFLUENCE OF HEGEL

Modern French philosophy, aside from the dominance of Jean-Paul Sartre and Existentialism, spent much of its intellectual energies with a rereading of the German philosopher Georg Wilhelm Friedrich Hegel (1770–1831). Hegel's book *The Phenomenology of Spirit* had been translated into French by Jean Hyppolite from 1939 to 1941. Two massively influential books had followed: Hyppolite's own commentary, *Genesis and Structure of Hegel's Phenomenology of Spirit* (1946) and Alexandre Kojève's lecture series at the Sorbonne (given 1933–1939), published as *Introduction to the Reading of Hegel* (1947). John Heckman, the translator of the English edition of Hyppolite's book, argues that:

> ... although the postwar period is usually associated with the triumph of "existentialism" in the persons of Jean-Paul Sartre and Maurice Merleau-Ponty, the moment of existentialism's triumph was also, in proper Hegelian form, the moment of its death. For the famous manifesto of the first number of *Les temps modernes* in October 1945, signaled a turn by Sartre and Merleau-Ponty away from Edmund Husserl and Martin Heidegger and towards Hegel and Marx.
>
> (Hyppolite, 1974: xvi)

It could be argued that Hyppolite, with his translation and commentary, was one of the most influential teachers of Hegel; some of the most powerful poststructuralists (see p. 16) – Gilles Deleuze, Jacques Derrida and Michel Foucault – studied under Hyppolite. So why was Hegel so important? This will prove crucial to our understanding of Baudrillard, especially as it could be argued that his countering of Marx parallels Bataille's earlier countering of Hegel.

Without doubt, the main reason for the interest in Hegel was the fact that his philosophy, and especially the notion of the *dialectic*, had heavily influenced Marxism, which was one of the dominant political movements in postwar France.

DIALECTIC

The Oxford Dictionary of Philosophy defines dialectic as "... a historical force, driving events onwards towards a progressive resolution of the contradictions that characterize each historical epoch" (Blackburn, 1996: 104). The word "dialectic" derives from Greek, and means "to converse", leading through philosophy to logical argumentation, where two opposing arguments or positions are "solved" by a third. This "third" argument or position becomes a new starting point for a further logical argument, and so the dialectic continues, ever driving forwards. Marxism combines Hegelian dialectics (or Hegel's dialectical insights into the formation of the human subject) with the insights of historical materialism. To put this another way, Hegel's theories of social structures are linked with economics, to show how societies evolve through class struggle.

According to Marxism, the end result of the dialectic is not Hegel's notion of Absolute Spirit (or philosophy), but societies' attainment of communism.

MARXISM

Karl Marx (1818–1883) and Friedrich Engels (1820–1895) published *The Communist Manifesto* in 1848 with the opening assertion that "The history of all hitherto existing society is the history of class struggles." Both men produced a number of key texts, but it was Marx's *Das Kapital* (first of three volumes published 1867) that became the mainstay for the political movement called Marxism. Marxism theorizes that economics is the determining factor in class struggle, and that Capitalism ultimately needs to be overthrown to liberate the working classes, who are maintained in a position of dependency to the industrialized state.

It needs to be stressed that, with Hegel's dialectic, politics and philosophy intersect. We can explore this in one of the most famous passages of Hegel's *Phenomenology of Spirit* – the master/slave section. Here, Hegel is concerned with self-consciousness, and the fact that the human subject can only be recognized as such through *another* human subject. The problem arises when "primitive" human beings demand recognition without return; the strong individual wants to be recognized as human, without realizing that such a recognition is universal (Taylor, 1989: 153). For example, we could have a person who demands that others recognize his basic human rights; but the person then fails to award the same human rights to those "others"! Hegel argues that at a primitive stage in their development this leads to a struggle between two human subjects, which ends for one of them in death. But here the problems begin: if the struggle had not taken place, recognition would always have remained "outside" of the human subject, in the other human subject. But, with the death of one of the combatants, there is no active recognition from that other subject, who no longer exists. What is the solution to this conundrum? It would appear to be the "giving in" of one of the combatants in the struggle to death, so, instead of losing their life, they lose freedom and become a

slave. The "master" now has a subject who recognizes his or her superiority and therefore identity. Charles Taylor writes that: "The full
relation of master and slave has to be understood with the aid of a third
term, material reality" (1989: 154). In other words, the master
consumes his or her surroundings, the material goods that the slave
produces through hard struggle. As Taylor says: "The master's experience is of the lack of solid reality … of things; the slave is the one who
experiences their independence and resistance as he works them"
(1989: 154). Ironically, this puts the slave in a potentially superior
position, because the master is recognized by a human being who has
no other recognition than through material things. This becomes an
indirect and "empty" recognition for the master, who wants to be
recognized, crudely speaking, by someone of the same stature. The
master has won and lost at the same time. The slave exists through and
for the master, and thus has a kind of indirect recognition, but one that
is also structured by the fear of death and the discipline of unending
work (1989: 154). Taylor argues that:

> The short, three-page … passage in which Hegel deals with this is one of the
> most important in the *Phenomenology of Spirit*, for the themes are not only
> essential to Hegel's philosophy but have had a longer career in an altered form
> in Marxism. The underlying idea, that servitude prepares the ultimate liberation
> of the slaves, and indeed general liberation, is recognizably preserved in
> Marxism. But the Marxist notion of the role of work is also foreshadowed here.
>
> (Taylor, 1989: 154–155)

The fear of death, for the slave, makes him or her aware of his situation, while the master becomes preoccupied with a passive
consumption; the transformation of his or her material reality through
work makes the slave aware that he can change his world, in comparison with the master's passivity. These two tied together – the fear of
death and world-transformation through work – initiate the true self-
consciousness that will lead to the slave's ultimate liberation. As Hegel
argues, it is through work that the slave discovers a mind of his or her
own, and that mind can be used to transform the slave's world in the
ways that he or she desires.

Hegel's dialectic is a voracious thing: it is all-encompassing, all-
consuming. The philosopher Martin Heidegger (1889–1976) argued
that the magnificence of the dialectic was because it *wasn't* something

like a mill, into which we pour our intellectual problems to be solved by the operation of thesis, antithesis, synthesis (the individual "moments" of the dialectic). Rather, our intellectual problems are made apparent to us through, or because of, the workings of the dialectic (another way of putting this is that the dialectic means we can think in the first place) (Heidegger, 1988: 112). Put this way, it has an uncanny knack of preceding and answering all intellectual movements and ideas. So, with the master/slave narrative, the dialectic does not somehow end or finish with the above outcome. Instead, we move on to the next stage in human existence, where the dialectical process starts all over again (we could say: the dialectic never rests). This is where, for thinkers such as Bataille and Baudrillard, the bigger problems begin. How are we to think "outside" the dialectic? If it is a process that never ends, you could say that there is no outside. How are we to counter such an imposing, all-consuming philosophical system? Perhaps the question might be: If it is such a successful system, why might we want to counter it? A quick answer would suggest that thinkers such as Bataille and Baudrillard are suspicious of totalizing systems of thought – they argue that there are experiences in the world that cannot be subsumed by the dialectic, and somehow operate at its limits, working (potentially) to fracture the entire system, just as a small crack in a large bell can ultimately destroy the entire structure.

BATAILLE VS HEGEL

In relation to this reading of Hegel, we can turn to the essay "The Notion of Expenditure", where Bataille tries to find a fracturing process. He argues that modern society is utilitarian, with two main strands of activity: the production and conservation of goods, and the reproduction and conservation of human life (Bataille, 1985: 116). Consumption must be conservative, not excessive, if it is to fit in with this ethos. However, Bataille recognizes two categories of consumption: the minimum consumption needed to continue the individual's productive life and that of "unproductive expenditures", of which we are given some examples: "luxury, mourning, war, cults, the construction of sumptuary monuments, games, spectacles, arts, perverse sexual activity …". Bataille argues that all of these activities have "no end beyond themselves" (1985: 118). A good example is Peter Weiss' play *Marat/Sade*, which Baudrillard translated in 1965. Cohen comments on

"the play's turbulent sequence of dance, pantomime, songs, and lita-
nies, performing acrobats, heroic tableaux, and by its displays of heated
revolutionary rhetoric disrupted by scenes of grotesque violence and
sexual excess" (Cohen, 1998: xiv). Its scenes of violence and excess are
not arbitrary, rather they are linked to the Marquis de Sade's eigh-
teenth-century anti-Enlightenment drive, replacing the highest values
of knowledge and reason with eroticism. So what we have with expenditure and "unproductive activity" is a notion that might be resistant to
totalizing systems such as the dialectic, because wasteful activity is
difficult to bring back "within" rigid systems of thought and behaviour.
At the very least, expenditure brings us to the limits of the dialectic.

Bataille's most famous example of the notion of expenditure is that
of the Canadian northwest coast native process called the potlatch. The
potlatch is a ceremony that usually takes place at transitional moments
such as puberty, weddings and funerals. The fundamental process
involves the giving of excessive gifts to the attendees, gifts that have
considerable value. Bataille notes that:

> Potlatch excludes all bargaining and, in general, is constituted by a consider-
> able gift of riches, offered openly and with the goal of humiliating, defying and
> obligating a rival. The exchange value of the gift results from the fact that the
> donee, in order to efface the humiliation and respond to the challenge, must
> satisfy the obligation (incurred by him at the time of acceptance) to respond
> later with a more valuable gift, in other words to return with interest.
>
> (1985: 121)

What interests Bataille is the fact that giving is not the only component
in the potlatch; a more powerful act is that of the destruction of
wealth, which reunites the potlatch "... with religious sacrifice, since
what is destroyed is theoretically offered to the mythical ancestors of
the donees" (1985: 121).

Clearly, this is not a system which reaches the ideal of non-exchange
and thus anti-utilitarianism, or a kind of pure loss (which presumably
would halt the dialectic in its tracks). Instead, it is one which *operates at
the limits* of the utilitarian, crossing back and forth between the
economic and the uneconomic, the rational and the spiritual, the
productive and the unproductive. Thus Bataille notes how wealth is not
ultimately lost by the potlatch, but actually inflated (it works like
credit in this sense); but such inflation of wealth is as it were a side

effect of the institution of potlatch, and it is not the result when physical destruction takes place because there is spiritual, not material, gain: "... wealth appears as an acquisition to the extent that power is acquired by a rich man, but it is entirely directed toward loss in the sense that this power is characterized as power to lose. It is only through loss that glory and honor are linked to wealth" (1985: 122).

Baudrillard recognizes Bataille as a key thinker who can go beyond the strictures of Hegel and Marx not in a simplistic sense of "opposing" Hegel or Marx (because then as an "antithesis" such opposition can be subsumed by the dialectic to reach a "higher" position which has conserved the original values in the process), but in the more radical, creative sense of working at the limits of Hegelian and/or Marxist thought. Later, we will see how Baudrillard uses the notion of expenditure or waste (*dépense*) in his book *Consumer Society*, and how the potlatch relates to the notion of "symbolic exchange" (see Chapter 3).

INFLUENCE OF MAY 1968 AND VIETNAM

The interest in Bataille amongst French thinkers signalled a wider interest in anthropology. Behind Bataille's notion of expenditure or waste, we find a work of anthropology by Marcel Mauss (1872–1950) called *The Gift*. And with the move of French thought away from Sartre because of a reaction against authorized modes of political thought, we find the structuralist anthropologist Claude Lévi-Strauss (1908–). In 1958, Lévi-Strauss had published a book which many would claim as deeply influential – the book was called *Anthropologie structurale* (*Structural Anthropology*), a manifesto for a movement that would gain rapid strength.

STRUCTURALISM

An intellectual movement that paid particular attention to the theories of Ferdinand de Saussure (1857–1913), who made a number of key assertions in a lecture series delivered at the University of Geneva, published posthumously as the *Cours de linguistique générale* (1915; published in English 1971). Saussure argued that the sign was composed of a signifier ("sound-image") and signified ("concept"). His key point, however, was that signs *do not* stand in for things, or objects in the world, and that the connection between a sign, such as "cat", and the object in the world, such as a furry domestic animal, is arbitrary. What this means is that the sign functions, or works for us, because it is part of a *system* of signs. The system generates or "makes" meaning, and it does this through difference. In other words, the sign "cat" has a meaning because in the system we call "language", it is different from the sign "dog". Note that we do not have to discuss furry domestic animals to think about the generation of meaning here. Structuralists are interested in the way that sign-systems work. There are many sign-systems to explore, from advertising to culinary systems (different cultural approaches to food). However, structuralists usually go beyond the "semiotic" level of signs themselves, to think about the way such systems function in the world, in relation to other issues such as ideology or philosophy. Also, the structuralist approach can be taken to mean a general interest in systems, or a way of perceiving cultural artefacts, events and theories *as* systems. For example, the early works of the famous French theorist Michel Foucault (1926–1984) were widely regarded as structuralist, although he strenuously denied this.

POSTSTRUCTURALISM

If Saussure had identified some radical ways of thinking about language and signs (e.g. meaning is "arbitrary"), it was the poststructuralist thinkers Derrida, Foucault and Lacan who examined the impact or effect of this radicality upon the world. Derrida examined the philosophical attitudes to writing and issued his infamous statement that "there is nothing outside the text"; Foucault examined the histories of madness, incarceration and sexuality, to show the links between power and knowledge; and Lacan re-read Sigmund Freud (the inventor of psychoanalysis), theorizing the "mirror stage" and the importance of the symbolic. Followers of these and other continental theorists are loosely termed "poststructuralist"; their ideas came to the fore in the 1980s with the rise of "theory" in university humanities departments.

In a cartoon sketch by Maurice Henry published in *La Quinzaine Littéraire* in 1967, we see four central structuralist thinkers: Michel Foucault, Jacques Lacan (1901–1981), Claude Lévi-Strauss and Roland Barthes (1915–1980). The last two were the men who would be considered structuralist through and through; the first two were heavily influenced by structuralist theories, and are known as *poststruc-turalists* because of this influence and the fact that they then went beyond it. Foucault, in his early work, claimed affinities which he would later deny, and Lacan, the psychoanalytical thinker, used struc-turalism to produce his seminar series published as *Écrits*. Didier Eribon notes that, since the beginning of the 1960s in France,

> ... every issue of every intellectual review not dedicated entirely to it had contained at least some mention of structuralism: structuralism and Marxism, structuralism against Marxism, structuralism and existentialism, structuralism against existentialism. Some promoted it; some opposed it; some were deter-mined to come up with a synthesis. Everybody, in every area of intellectual life, took a position. Rarely had culture bubbled and seethed with more intensity.
>
> (1991: 160)

One of the key issues which culture "bubbled and seethed" about was that of the "system". Lacan had argued that the unconscious was struc-tured like a language, and it would generally be agreed within structuralist circles that the human subject is born into systems of meaning. This is a reversal of what is known as the liberal humanist position, where the human subject has "essential" qualities, and "genius" that can generate significant meanings or works of art which project such essentiality. Another way of thinking about this position is in rela-tion to biographical criticism, which often argues that all the "meaning" in a series of novels or paintings, for example, can be traced back to the person who constructed them. The structuralist position would argue that human beings are already part of systems of thought that enable them to construct various works, and so on. If the system precedes the subject, then the liberal humanist genius or more general conception of "man" is effaced, "like a face drawn in sand at the edge of the sea", as Foucault writes at the close of *The Order of Things* in 1966 (published in English 1974). Structuralism also rejects Hegelian tele-ology, or the notion that the signification of something is generated by its goal or end (a teleological system must keep moving forwards). Think about the fact that Baudrillard lived through the implementation of the Monnet Plans (see pp. 2–3) – they demanded that people direct their working lives according to a system. The French subject would be defined through his or her relation to the Plans, which in turn had meaning because of their goal (modernization and greater productivity).

It is worth considering the fact that structuralist debates in the class-rooms and lecture theatres had a direct relation to changes in society, and that theorists such as Baudrillard would have experienced the knock-on effects of such changes in everyday life.

John Ardagh notes how the publication of Michel Foucault's *Les Mots et les choses* (*The Order of Things*) sent minor shockwaves throughout French society because of its perceived message replacing Nietzsche's and Sartre's atheistic approaches (the now notorious notion of the "death of God") with the "death of man" (1977: 549). Just as Sartre had attacked Lévi-Strauss, now Foucault would attack Sartre, saying that Sartre's "*La critique de la raison dialectique* is the magnificent and pathetic effort of a nineteenth-century man to conceive of the twentieth century" (Eribon, 1991: 161). Sartre's readings of literature and literary figures also came under attack, because he had interpreted fictional works in terms of political engagement. The new approach to literary criticism and structuralist or poststructuralist philosophical enquiry, which would later be simply called "theory", rejected the notion of "engagement" in a simplistic sense. Thus the critics gathered in the journal *Tel Quel* (1960–1983) would first move away from Sartre simply by focusing on literature, and then arguing that "engagement" could be read at the level of form (Ffrench, 1995: 35). During this period, academic disputes gained notoriety and newspaper headlines. For example, the dispute between Roland Barthes and Raymond Picard (a Sorbonne lecturer) was essentially about the differences between traditional literary approaches and the new theory. However, "theory" as such was not completely uniform and homogeneous: it, too, had its divisions, and they would become clearer as the 1960s progressed. The "clash of cultures" would be repeated from another perspective in 1968, with the question:

> ... as to whether the "spontaneous" and "active" uprising of May 1968 had, or had not, disproved the whole determinist basis [that choices are made in advance because of a system] of structuralism. Anti-structuralists eagerly seized on the May explosion as a chance to refute a philosophy they hated.
>
> (Ardagh, 1977: 550)

Baudrillard was teaching at Nanterre at the time of the 1968 student uprising – exactly where it started, putting him, to use Mike Gane's phrase, "at the centre of the brewing storm" (Gane, 1993: 2). At this time Baudrillard was questioning Marxism from a structuralist perspective, the latter being applied in his 1968 thesis publication *The System of Objects*. So which side of the structuralist debate does Baudrillard argue from in May 1968? Can we analyse whether May 1968 refutes or confirms the structuralist position, providing Baudrillard with a model to work from, or with, in later analyses and publications?

VIETNAM

As noted, in 1968 Baudrillard published a French translation of Weiss' play *Discours sur la genèse et le déroulement de la très longue guerre de libération du Vietnam*, translated into English as the slightly less unwieldy *Discourse on Vietnam* (translated by Geoffrey Skelton in 1970). Weiss' play was a powerful, Marxist condemnation of the war in Vietnam, directly implicating and attacking American involvement. Unlike the complex aesthetics of expenditure found in *Marat/Sade*, in this play Weiss suggests that the capitalist system expends or "wastes" economic surplus to defend its own imperialist regime. The play does not just condemn American aggression in Vietnam, it also highlights the fact that this was the first real "television" war. Through the media, the propaganda machine was brought into conflict with the dissemination of critical, anti-war perspectives. We will turn to Baudrillard's commentary on the media and May 1968 below (see pp. 21–24). For the moment, we can see how Weiss' play embodies the position taken by activists and especially student activists across the world as the Vietnam War (1959–1973) became an international issue. Some commentators have argued that this international sense of student revolt and rejection of authority embodied by attitudes towards the US led to more local or national unrest, such as we find in France. Others have argued that more mundane issues were primarily responsible for local activity. Maurice Larkin notes that an opinion poll of French students taken in November 1968 "... revealed that 56 per cent believed that the May upheavals essentially represented anxiety over future employment, 35 per cent felt that inadequate university facilities were primarily to blame, while only 12 per cent saw it as an attempt to transform society" (1991: 318). Perhaps another way of formulating this opinion poll is in relation to the way an idealizing, modernizing, force in French society had come up against the archaic structures of a previous age: nowhere was this more apparent than in the education system.

EDUCATION AND REVOLUTION

Belated educational reforms in line with the modernizing society came most forcefully in 1965, with the work of the Minister for Education, Christian Fouchet. The main impetus was in the realm of the *baccalauréat*, which was the highly academic passport to university and later employment. The main criticism of the *baccalauréat* was that it was too rigid in terms of subject matter and left students who failed it without vocational training. Fouchet was largely responsible for updating the *baccalauréat*, removing huge chunks of philosophical material and updating it with modern subjects such as economics and sociology (Ardagh, 1977: 469–470). The *baccalauréat* system did, however, guarantee entrance to university if a student passed, unlike the more selective procedures found in countries such as Britain, and this in turn led to extensive drop-out rates amongst undergraduate students. Between 1967 and 1968, for example, France had increased its student number by 56,000, to over 500,000, but the failure rate was over 50 per cent (Larkin, 1991: 318–319). The student numbers may have expanded, but institutional resources, buildings, materials and new teachers were all lagging behind. New universities were constructed, as well as an "overspill" campus for Paris University, called Nanterre, where Baudrillard taught from 1966. The environment at Nanterre has been described as bleak and inhuman, "a desert of glass and steel" (Ardagh, 1977: 501). It was the political activists studying there who really shook the place up: Daniel Cohn-Bendit is the name most frequently cited in relation to the unrest at Nanterre amongst the Anarchist, Trotskyite and Maoist groups. With the 1968 attempted assassination of the German student radical leader Rudi Dutschke by right-wingers in Berlin, student unrest exploded. Nanterre militants moved their activities to the Sorbonne after the closure of Nanterre on 2 May (Larkin, 1991: 320). Was student unrest the sign of a bigger, possibly global, desire for political revolution? Would this put to rest structuralist notions of powerfully embedded systems that organize society? Most commentators note how the mainly middle-class student uprising did intersect with working-class concerns to a certain extent. But this intersection was short-lived and never really anything more, as

Cohn-Bendit suggested, with his "revolutionary detonation" theory (Larkin, 1991: 321). In other words, the student uprising would "trigger" or initiate a series of bigger political events, which in itself suggests that the students and workers were not as coordinated as television pictures of the unrest might have made apparent. This is not to say that strikes on a vast scale did not occur; as Larkin notes, "... by 20th May a large segment of the private sector was also in the grip of a general strike, and overall numbers escalated within a few days to a staggering ten million" (1991: 323). Riot police engaged in aggressive tactics, and public unrest intensified. By 24 May, riots and demonstrations were occurring throughout France, not just the capital. It would be accurate to say that the student uprising of 1968 coincided with more general concerns in the country, such as the 1967 recession and the rise in unemployment numbers; union action increased to the boiling point of 1968. But the workers were demanding something quite different from the radical student activists, who were arguing, crudely speaking, for conditions that the workers never really felt applied to them: better educational conditions, and/or widespread political revolution. The unions wanted everyday conditions to improve for their members, and the political backlash in June, with de Gaulle's triumphant reaffirmation of power, came after the return of most workers to the factory floor (Larkin, 1991: 323–327).

Baudrillard comments upon the 1968 uprising in a chapter called "Requiem for the Media" in his book *For a Critique of the Political Economy of the Sign* (1972). He calls the transgressive student action at Nanterre in May "symbolic":

> ... at a given time in a given place, an act of radical rupture was invented – or ... a particular response was invented there, where the institutions of administrative and pedagogical power were engaged in a private *oratoria* and functioned precisely to interdict any answer.
>
> (1981: 174)

Baudrillard is suggesting here that the university is a site of knowledge transmission, with no inbuilt space for exchanges of views or alternative positions. Indeed, in relation to this, one of the key concerns with the *baccalauréat* system leading up to university was that it was so intense, with such a large volume of material to be passed on to the students, that the teacher primarily became a one-way street of information, with little or no dialogue in the classroom or elsewhere, e.g. social events or sports. Baudrillard, however, is pointing to a wider conception of the ideological problems involved in the university system, which functions in the pre-1968 scenario by a code that denies response or exchange at a fundamental level (in other words, instead of being the result of a problem, like the *baccalauréat*, the problem is "inbuilt"). The events at Nanterre are "symbolic" because they "rupture" this transmission of the code; they not only disrupt the economy of learning, but they attempt to install dialogue instead of the academic monologues they replace. The "symbolic" is a notion which functions like Bataille's "waste" or "excess" – the notion of *expenditure* that attempts to fracture the Hegelian dialectic. The excessive nature of the student unrest generates a large part of its effects: it is extremely spectacular in its disruption and "destruction" of normal everyday society. The "event" itself is symbolic, not the larger-scale series of events or "results", which the media and others then try and control through their interpretations.

Baudrillard asks: What was the role of the media in the 1968 uprising? He argues that the naïve position is to conceive of the media as either oppressive and in need of reform (even taking over), or as helping the political unrest by spreading or disseminating the political message. Both of these positions are, according to him, simply incorrect. He states:

> May '68 will serve well enough as an example. Everything would lead us to believe in the subversive impact of the media during this period. Suburban radio stations and newspapers spread the student action everywhere. If the students were the detonators, the media were the resonators. Furthermore, the authorities quite openly accused the media of "playing the revolutionary game." ... I would say to the contrary that the media have never discharged their responsibilities with more efficiency, and that ... in their function of habitual social control, they were right on top of the action.
>
> (1981: 173)

What is wrong with the media disseminating knowledge of the events? The answer is that what should have a "natural" rhythm – the unfolding of a complex number of actions as people make their own decision to join the students – is vastly accelerated by the media. The media is interested only in a singular image of "revolution" which can be reproduced endlessly; in acceleration and reproduction of the singular, the complexities of events on the street are "short-circuited" and thus degraded. Further, the type of communicative exchange that Baudrillard idealizes at Nanterre and on the streets is *apparently* available via the media: but this is an illusion, since the media "... *are what always prevents response*, making all processes of exchange impossible ... except in the various forms of response simulation, themselves integrated in the transmission process ..." (1981: 170). In other words, the media itself is a one-way street, or its form is analogous to precisely those educational structures that the students were reacting against. In discussing the power of such a one-way street, Baudrillard refers in passing, without explaining further, to how in "primitive" societies, power belongs to those who give but cannot be repaid; we will come back to this below (and clearly we can think about this intersection or economy of power/knowledge in relation to the work of Foucault). Does Baudrillard give an example of a media which escapes all of these problems? In a passage which is regarded by many critics as naïve, and perhaps slightly absurd (given his later work), Baudrillard does make some suggestions:

> The real revolutionary media during May were the walls and their speech, the silk-screen posters and the hand-painted notices, the street where speech began and was exchanged – everything that was an *immediate* inscription, given and returned, spoken and answered, mobile in the same space and time, reciprocal and antagonistic. The street is, in this sense, the alternative and subversive form of the mass media, since it isn't, like the latter, an objectified support for answerless messages, a transmission system at a distance.
>
> (1981: 176)

Thus, to try and take over (or reverse the processes) of the media is futile, because its form remains the same, and that is precisely what Baudrillard is analysing here. Baudrillard, like Bataille, is interested in the marginal reaching of the limits, where institutionalized structures are shaken and possibly destroyed. In Baudrillard's later work on postmodernism, we will see this optimism fade, although limits are still discussed and explored.

In using elements of structural analysis and anthropological knowledge to analyse the role of the media during May 1968, Baudrillard is suggesting that the structuralist vs Marxism oppositional question is too simply put. Rejecting simplistic political models of "overturning", Baudrillard in the process also critiques contemporary communication theory. Many of the issues that occur later in Baudrillard's work are already present here, such as the notion of simulation (see Chapter 5), where the media are "simulating" audience or "participant" response (e.g. the so-called "public referendum"). We could argue that, while Baudrillard clearly values a communicative situation that *ruptures* simulation, with a return as such to symbolic exchange relating to premodern (or "primitive") society, he is also aware of the anachronistic nature of such a rupture. The modernizing of France, in large part via the successive Monnet Plans, was by 1968 a virtually irreversible process. The Monnet Plans were themselves preprogrammed simulations of success: once launched into the public domain, it was up to "reality" to fall into line with the indicative future. Looking at Baudrillard's *System of Objects*, we can see how the new materials of modern France are those which would hardly have been noticed by Hegelians, existentialists and Marxists. As a thinker and writer working in the intersecting intellectual domains sketched out above, however, Baudrillard is able to locate the areas of contemporary life that are in need of analysis. Thus we find him meditating on modular furniture and glass, antiques, gadgets and robots, to pick just a few subjects from his 1968 publication. Perhaps it is here that we can trace an early interest in America; a technocratic France knew that it had much to learn from the most modern nation in the world, but the French also feared the possible damage to their own culture that could result from too close an involvement in the US (Ardagh, 1977: 704). The following chapter examines the central role of technology in Baudrillard's thought.

SUMMARY

We have seen in this chapter how the dominance of Hegel in postwar France led initially to the prevalence of Marxism and existentialism. Hyppolite, who translated Hegel, was also the teacher of some of the new thinkers, such as Derrida and Foucault. They were interested in different ways of intersecting reactions to Hegel with structuralism. A key figure for the new thinkers was Bataille, whose theories of "unproductive expenditure" and excessive behaviour were aimed at countering the Hegelian dialectic. Baudrillard regarded the political unrest of May 1968, with student and worker uprisings, as something that tested the opposing theories of Marxism and structuralism. He suggested that the two theories needed to be brought together, in the process identifying new areas of intellectual analysis in modern France.

SUMMARY

2

THE TECHNOLOGICAL
SYSTEM OF OBJECTS

One of the keys to Baudrillard's work is the analysis of technology explored in his first published book, *The System of Objects*, which is the focus here. This chapter first examines Baudrillard's notions of speed, "fuzzy" logic and automatism, and then goes on to examine the "gizmo" and the "gadget", thinking about the ways in which the technological object becomes designed according to human fantasy and desire. Technology is then related to some early versions of Baudrillard's notion of "the symbolic", and the argument concludes with a mapping out of the new technological space of the "hypermarket".

TECHNOLOGY

One of the key components that structures the postmodern world (or psyche) is technology. From the earliest science fiction novel, technology has stood in for the future, the radically new or different, and the obsession of all ultramodern societies. We define our societies by the technologies used, be that definition "stone age" or "computer age", and generally fit such descriptions into linear, progressive models of technological advancement. But we are also aware that narratives of progression rarely examine the fuzzy edges of technology – the built-in redundancy of consumer objects, the ways in which outmoded medicines and military technologies are offloaded to the Developing World, the ways in which ideological battles are supported (or generated) by technology races, from the Cold War to Star Wars (SDI), and so on. While there is a disjunction in the West between those who embrace new technologies (e.g. the current expansion of genetic engineering in crops) and those who reject them (e.g. the rise in the eco-protester), such a massive either/or binary fracturing rarely goes beyond the grand narratives of technology as redemptive (saving the world) or apocalyptic (destroying the world). Some theorists have argued that postmodernity itself splits into those who support "soft" and "hard" technologies; the former may involve a return to premodern agricultural practices synthesized with the best in contemporary knowledge of crop production, the latter may involve a vision of a cybernetic future, where the merging of organic and artificial worlds is achieved through new computer technologies. All of these options and concepts of technology have fascinated Baudrillard, especially the ways in which the subject experiences technology as part of everyday life in the present. It goes without saying that Baudrillard critiques the grand narratives of technological progression *and* apocalypse, preferring instead to map out in minute detail the impact of technological objects. In Chapter 4, we will discuss the shift in Baudrillard's work from notions of production to those of consumption and the way in which this leads to a critique of Marxism. In this chapter we will examine the role technological objects have played in Baudrillard's work, especially in relation to the transition from modern to postmodern society.

MODERNISM

An artistic movement that began at the turn of the twentieth century, and was heavily influenced by the events and experiences of World War I (1914–1918). In the art world there were many modernist movements, including Cubism, Futurism, Vorticism, Surrealism and Primitivism. All of these movements reflected the new ways that human beings existed in, and experienced, an industrialized, technological world. For example, Cubism fractures or shatters the human form, while Futurism celebrates the speed of the factory production line and the automobile. In literature, modernists were intensely interested in Sigmund Freud's psychoanalysis, and explored the interior subjectivity with new techniques such as interior monologue and stream of consciousness. Key authors include T.S. Eliot (*The Waste Land*), James Joyce (*Ulysses*) and Virginia Woolf (*Mrs Dalloway* and *To the Lighthouse*).

EMERGENCE OF A CONSUMER SOCIETY

One of Baudrillard's most sustained analyses of technological objects occurs in *The System of Objects*. But it would be a mistake to read this analysis in terms of comments on postmodernism. In *The System of Objects* Baudrillard is looking at the emergence of consumer society in the newly modernized or "modern" France. America is a model for France at this stage, but it is still a fairly distant one, without the immediacy of the later texts. Further, Baudrillard is still deeply concerned with other models – those of production – and he has yet to work out a more coherent theory of consumption. In many respects it is as if he is mapping out the consumer world in advance of the critique of Marxism, and it is in the *process* of "mapping" that the tools for that critique will be found.

Using a fairly traditional notion of the shift towards automatism, Baudrillard starts to theorize the modern, mechanistic object. In looking at the craze for antiques, Baudrillard notes how whatever is lacking in the human subject is invested in the object (1997: 82). For example, someone who desires social status might buy a stately home, or, on a smaller scale, the art objects that would be found in a stately home, such as "ancestral" portraits, which the new owner passes off as belonging to his or her own family. There is a further complication, though: the form of the object is not necessarily related to its utilitarian function. In the example of the huge American cars of the 1950s, with massive "tail fins", the fins themselves represent speed, but in actuality are counterproductive in terms of drag and the real velocity attainable – the fins are thus representative of a fantasy of aerodynamics (e.g. based upon the shape of aeroplanes):

Tail fins were a sign not of *real* speed but of a sublime, measureless speed. They suggested a miraculous automatism, a sort of grace. It was the presence of these fins that in our imagination propelled the car, which, thanks to them, seemed to fly along of its own accord ...

(1997: 59)

The speed generated by these fins is thus "absolute"; that is, speed which can never degenerate into the real because it belongs to the abstracted hyperreal.

HYPERREAL

Baudrillard argues that there are three levels of simulation, where the first level is an obvious copy of reality and the second level is a copy so good that it blurs the boundaries between reality and representation. The third level is one which produces a reality of its own without being based upon any particular bit of the real world. The best example is probably "virtual reality", which is a world generated by computer languages or code. Virtual reality is thus a world generated by mathematical models which are abstract entities. It is this third level of simulation, where the model comes before the constructed world, that Baudrillard calls the hyperreal.

An example of "absolute" speed is the contemporary public-road "sports car", which actually goes slower than, or at the same speed as, a turbo-charged family saloon; the family saloon *looks* like the slower of the two and would never be owned by someone who wants to be identified as "living in the fast lane". The latter person has bought into the "absolute" speed represented by the *form* of his or her vehicle, not the actual performance on the motorway or when stuck in heavy traffic in the city. The wider point that Baudrillard is making is that the "miraculous automatism" represented by the functionally useless tail fins is seriously counterproductive, yet becomes a necessity for the consumer via the manufacturer's promise that here is something progressively "better" to own (these tail fins are bigger so this car is closer to fulfilling your dreams). Automatism is presented to the consumer as technological progression, whereas Baudrillard immediately critiques it, with reference to what now seems like an incredibly archaic example: the shift from the automobile starting handle to battery-operated ignition. Baudrillard argues that this shift unnecessarily complicates the automobile as machine, making it dependent upon a battery which is "external" to the mechanical system, making it more prone to failure – e.g. a dead battery means that the car cannot be easily started – and simply more complicated. However, in terms of the grand narrative of technological progression, cars with starting handles now seem hilariously outmoded and outdated, belonging to distant memories of Keystone Cops movies and museum pieces, whereas electronic ignition is a marker of the modern. The grand narrative, which touts automatism as the vector of progression, subordinates "real" functionality to the stereotype of functionality. What Baudrillard means by this is that the ideal of abstracted automatism – e.g. perfected distant ease of use and ideal speed – dictates how the machine will be built, even if it means sacrificing some other improvement or radical design difference. As an example of this we can think about the way in which manufacturers resisted the introduction of unleaded petrol in Britain, which belonged to another forthcoming grand narrative, that of environmental and ecological protection.

"FUZZY" LOGIC

The next shift in the technological object that Baudrillard discusses is that of "indeterminacy", or the fuzzy logic which allows a machine to respond to random outside information (1997: 111). Instead of the closed systems that automatism generates in the example of the abstracted teleology of the automobile, indeterminate machines are open-ended systems. An example of such an open-ended system might be an environmentally friendly temperature control system in an office building that responds automatically to changes in the weather rather than needing internal, human control. However, such a system is still dominated by the abstract ideal of automatism (the building works by itself), however open to change it might be, and it is this aspect of the technological object that Baudrillard argues gives the subject the most pleasure: "For the user, automatism means a wondrous absence of activity, and the enjoyment this procures is comparable to that derived, on another plane, from seeing without being seen: an esoteric satisfaction experienced at the most everyday level" (1997: 111). The automated machine working away by itself and able to make basic decisions of its own is inevitably seen to be analogous to the subject, which becomes "a new anthropomorphism" (like a human being). Where earlier modern technologies were concerned with the utilitarian reproduction of more efficient tools and enclosing technologies, such as the office and home environment, the new anthropomorphic technologies are concerned with autonomous consciousness, abstracted power and identity. But, again, this may appear to be a radical step forwards in the grand narrative of progression, whereas in reality, for Baudrillard, this is another moment of standing still. Automatism now has the human subject as the ideal to be striving towards, and the human subject becomes the next barrier to the development of the technological object, because of the "oversignification" of the human subject:

> Man, for his part, by automating his objects and rendering them multi-functional instead of striving to structure his practices in a fluid and open-ended manner, reveals in a way what part he himself plays in a technical society: that of the most beautiful all-purpose object, that of an instrumental object.
>
> (1997: 112)

In other words, the subject not only blocks the development of the technological object but is revealed to be an object himself or herself within contemporary society.

FUNCTIONALITY

In the modern age, how functional are the technological objects that surround us? Have they penetrated our everyday practices to make a substantive difference to the way we lead our lives, or is this difference one of surface effect, ornamentation? Baudrillard announces in *The System of Objects* that in many respects it is the baroque that is the truly inaugurating moment of the modern age. In other words, there is no true development of the technological object, just a kind of abstraction (objects become mere lifestyle accessories), which Baudrillard equates with the architectural style of ornamentation that prevailed in Europe from the late sixteenth to early eighteenth centuries. In the contemporary world, the object is now taken over by the imaginary. Thus automatism "... opens the door to a whole world of functional delusion, to the entire range of manufactured objects in which a role is played by irrational complexity, obsessive detail, eccentric technicity or gratuitous formalism" (1997: 113). To say that technological objects exist as ornamentation at whatever level is not to say that they don't have a function; in fact, the opposite is the case. In the baroque world of technology, an object fulfils all the criteria for its usefulness simply by functioning in the abstract sense. For example, a more powerful computer may be used for the same simple word processing that was performed on an older machine that cost a lot less money. The machine's "power" is abstract in that it is not really tested out or used in any meaningful way. So we no longer have the question "What does it do?" but instead the question "Does it work?" This latter is what can be called a "hyperfunctionality", because other questions follow, such as "Does it work faster than the last model?", even if speed of operation has nothing to do with any real performance output or gain. In hyperfunctionality, the technological object is not practical, but obsessional; not utilitarian, but functional (always in an abstract sense): the object or gadget no longer serves the world, performing some useful task – it serves us: our dreams and desires of what objects can and should do (1997: 114). Baudrillard's word for this "empty functionalism" is the French word *machin*, meaning "thingumajig", "thingumabob", "whatsit" or, as the translator of *The System of Objects* more satisfactorily puts it, "gizmo" (1997: 114). The gizmo is an object that is not of any real or genuine use to anyone and it also lacks a specifying name. Any number of different objects can be "gizmos" (such as the plastic strips attached to the back of cars popular in the 1980s to "remove" static electricity), with no real scientific basis that they actually worked. This lack on behalf of language (or lag behind the trend continually to produce new gizmos) is perhaps representative of a conceptual lack, where the functioning of the gizmo becomes mysterious. The gizmo is a myth-making device because it operates not through clear logical reason, but according to the fragmented personal mythologies of the individual user – for example, the person who believes that an aeroplane only really stays in the sky during a flight due to their own intense concentration. In this fragmented sense of mystery and mythology the gizmo is "worse" than, say, a religious icon, which represents an ordered system of belief structured around an object. But is the gizmo therefore a degraded technological object, inferior to the machine? The answer according to Baudrillard is that it is not, because it is an object that operates in the imaginary rather than the real. We can see here a division between the real and the hyperreal which has yet to be fully theorized (see Chapter 5 for more detail). The gizmo is constructed according to the model of pure functioning, and a reality constructed via models only is a postmodern "hyperreality". Baudrillard suggests that the gizmo represents the belief in the universality of technological objects – this belief says that for every need there is a gizmo that will provide assistance, and thus nature itself becomes automated. What Baudrillard means by this can be thought through with the example he gives of the "... electrical whatsit that extracts stones from fruit ..." that some people may have as a kitchen gadget. We have all bought such gadgets, which purport to be incredibly useful but usually end up crammed in a cupboard gathering dust or used once or twice a year because we don't have space for the gizmo and it takes more effort to use the gizmo than remove fruit stones with a knife! However, Baudrillard's theoretical point is that the belief in the universal use of gizmos means that nature (the fruit stone and beyond) becomes something that gizmos can always work upon to improve. The belief that technology will always improve nature implies that nature is itself constructed like a technological device. In the process of automatism, the human subject universalizes itself as a functional being that can always find satisfaction through the gizmo, whereas the gizmo is bound up by that dream of functionality and thus reduced to the "...irrationality of human determinants" (1996: 116). There is a resistance to the former development, where people reject the interpenetration of subject and technology, but the latter, the imposition of the functional dream upon the possibilities of the technological object or gizmo, is rarely, if ever, theorized. The dream of a perfectly working functionality of the world is transferred to the ideal perfectly working body. While the Freudian strand of *The System of Objects* remains undeveloped, an interesting parallel between Baudrillard's notion here and the rise in popularity of "functionality drugs" such as Prozac and Viagra in the 1990s, would suggest a fairly prescient reading on his behalf.

The technological object, it becomes clear, does not according to Baudrillard embody the grand narratives of progression – instead, the technological object is restricted by its anthropomorphic fashioning, its interpenetration with the world of human fantasy and desire. In this sense, the object is dysfunctional, held back from "true" development, limited in its application and slotted into preprogrammed ideas. But this is not the only way in which Baudrillard theorizes the object as dysfunctional. With the example of the science fiction robot, which is placed in the "pure realm of the gizmo" (1997: 119), there is always a supplementary marker of difference, which foregrounds the fact that the robot is both the technological object perfected and a mechanical slave. A robot that reached its ideal would be able to do everything the human subject could, including reproduction of the species and, further, it would naturally efface the fact that it was a robot in the first place, because its mimetic capabilities would be that of second-order simulation. In other words, it would not be possible to distinguish between the original and the copy. Baudrillard notes that this attainment would lead to intense anxiety; such anxiety would be of the sort that Philip K. Dick so expertly manipulates in his novel *Do Androids Dream of Electric Sheep?*, now known through its film adaptation *Blade Runner*. However, the robot's supplementary markers of difference – a metallic skin, gestures which are "… discrete, jerky and unhuman", the ability to process data at an abnormal speed, and so on – all lead to the reassurance that the robot is not the human subject's double (1997: 120). The robot is a castrated slave, always seen as the attainment of perfection in terms of the technological object, but always falling short of the attainment of humanity and concrete subjectivity. In terms of its evolution, the robot is thus a dead end, and this is where for Baudrillard all objects in our consumer world now arrive.

THE END OF THE SYMBOLIC

Technology, for Baudrillard, is the compensatory mode of being in a world which has been deprived of the symbolic dimension. At times hovering close to nostalgia, but aware of the problematic of this way of thinking, Baudrillard argues that the relationship between the human subject and processes of symbolic ritualized behaviour (including work) has been divorced partly by the transference of gestural activity to technological objects. Instead of the human subject being in the world, it is now the object that is in the world, while the human subject has become an idle spectator. Worse still, the complexity of the world no longer occurs at the moment of symbolic exchange, such as the potlatch, but resides instead in the everyday life of the technological object (the object is more complex than the human subject and his or her social existence/structures). But are technological objects, even with their idealized functioning, completely divorced from the symbolic? What about the fetishism of objects? Surely that has a symbolic dimension? And, thinking of the ways in which Baudrillard depends so essentially on absolute expenditure and waste from the Eurocentric narratives of primitivism, surely one of the key markers of contemporary Western society is precisely wasteful expenditure? How can Baudrillard keep asserting the end of the symbolic in these instances?

PRIMITIVISM

An artistic movement that forms a part of modernism, but also an "attitude" held towards other, non-Western cultures. Artists interested in Primitivism used cultural artefacts from non-Western cultures, such as Africa and the Native Americas, to feed into avant-garde aesthetics, such as the use of Native masks in Cubism. Native peoples are seen via Primitivism as somehow closer to nature, naïve, "savage", and untouched by the rules and regulations of Western society. So-called "primitive" peoples were in reality often part of highly autonomous, complex societies, with their own forms of religion, politics and aesthetics (e.g. the First Nations of British Columbia, Canada).

Contemporary fetishism is analysed by Baudrillard in a number of places, although the most condensed account is found in *For a Critique of the Political Economy of the Sign*, where the Marxist notion of commodity fetishism comes in for some criticism (although, at this stage, for not saying enough about production). Baudrillard's thesis is that the word "fetishism" has a life of its own: instead of describing a *process* whereby an object is endowed with magical properties (e.g. the "primitive" fetish), the people who use the term are exposed in turn for using non-reflectively a "magical thinking" (1981: 90). Commodity fetishism is one of the grand narratives that is being teased apart here, whereby the shift from concrete production and exchange is replaced by abstracted labour relations and subsequent alienation. Fundamentally, however, the term "fetishism" is rejected because of the moral baggage it has carried since the Enlightenment: "... the whole repertoire of occidental Christian and humanist ideology, as orchestrated by colonists, ethnologists and missionaries" (1981: 88).

In other words, the term "fetishism" has been used not simply to describe "primitive" cultures and practices, but to condemn them, especially for the notion of worshipping "false idols". While Baudrillard doesn't mention that the rejection of fetishism is also an internal policing matter for monotheistic religion (the worship of one god that could potentially be disseminated and destroyed by an abundance of concrete images worshipped in His place), he does pick up on the way that fetishism has become a *metaphor* for the analysis of "magical thinking", be it "primitive" or "contemporary" (1981: 88). In anthropological analysis, there is a reversal that the analysts are themselves unaware of: "primitive" fetishism involves notions of energy transfer, capture and beneficial control by the tribal group. This process is called here a "'rationalization' of the world" (1981: 89). The reversal comes about by the suggestion that anthropologists are, in the process of their pseudo-scientific work, doing much the same thing with their subjects, containing the critical energy that is found in the so-called "primitive" society. This criticism parallels that found in Wittgenstein's "Remarks on Fraser's *Golden Bough*", discussed briefly in Chapter 3. The reversal can be applied, furthermore, to "modern industrial society":

> What else is intended by the concept of "commodity fetishism" if not the

notion of a false consciousness devoted to the worship of exchange value (or, more recently, the fetishism of gadgets or objects, in which individuals are supposed to worship artificial libidinal or prestige values incorporated in the object)?

(Baudrillard, 1981: 89)

In other words, it is not a case of saying that exchange-value is fetishistic and thus false, in turn revealing that use-value underlies such alienation; rather, all fetishistic activity is based upon the fascination of signs. Instead of perceiving the contemporary fetish for consumer objects or the body as something with symbolic value, the whole process is here perceived as emptied of value:

... the subject is trapped in the factitious, differential, encoded, systematized aspect of the object. It is not the passion (whether of objects or subjects) for substances that speaks in fetishism, it is the *passion for the code*, which by governing both objects and subjects, and by subordinating them to itself, delivers them up to abstract manipulation. This is the fundamental articulation of the ideological process: not in the projection of alienated consciousness into various superstructures, but in the generalization at all levels of a structural code.

(1981: 92)

With the current obsession for ever more powerful technological gizmos and gadgets, with their almost instantly built-in obsolescence (such as personal computers that are not powerful enough to run the "latest" software), a huge number of such objects are doomed not for actual use but fairly rapid disposal: such objects are waste. Even as we go out to buy our latest gizmo, or boast about its "configuration", we know that the gizmo is doomed: *tomorrow brings the next upgraded model*. Our consumption is simultaneously *destruction*, however long we try to put off the fateful moment. (We are also aware that a small, bizarre, group of people are infinitely putting off buying their gizmo precisely because the next model will be more powerful and less expensive; as such these people step permanently outside of the circuit of consumption as waste and waste as consumption, living in a strangely archaic world.) It is not just at the personal level that objects are "wasted": the biggest waste of all in Western society comes via expenditure on the latest military technology. Military objects have an analogous life span of zero (they are inevitably outmoded the moment they come off the production line), with the added advantage that they can be destroyed, exhausted, worn out, and so on, on the battlefield, or sold to the Developing World. The huge disparity between Western and non-Western military technology does cause problems (war becomes too easy, so to speak), and this leads to hyperreal wars as discussed in the chapters on postmodernism (Chapters 5, 6 and 7). But does either this personal or public expenditure have any symbolic value?

In *The Consumer Society* (1988b), Baudrillard asserts that not only does the Western world need its objects to construct an identity but, more fundamentally, it needs to destroy those objects. Thus the shift in the media from interest in heroes of production to heroes of consumption, or, as Baudrillard puts it, those "dinosaurs" whose excessively wasteful lives dominate popular culture. But there is also a more cautionary, moralistic message that says that excessive, wasteful consumption is "bad", damaging to the environment (but not the economy). Waste in this latter sense is seen as the excessive, insane action of subjects living for the present, damaging irreparably a finite reserve of common resources. Clearly, in *The Consumer Society*, this moralistic analysis of waste comes under suspicion and is reviewed with a "sociological" analysis, suggesting that excessive consumption is a universal. Referring to the potlatch and the wasteful expenditure of the aristocratic classes, the suggestion is that contemporary utilitarianism needs to be re-evaluated in terms of this universal:

> … waste, far from being an irrational residue, takes on a positive function, taking over where rational utility leaves off to play its part in a higher social functionality – a social logic in which waste even appears ultimately as the essential function, the extra degree of expenditure, superfluity, the ritual uselessness of "expenditure for nothing" becoming the site of production of values, differences and meanings on both the individual and the social level.
>
> (1998b: 43)

The reversal here indicates that, rather than having a society which sees excessive consumption as morally bad, consumption as consummation becomes "the good". To make sense of this, Baudrillard first asks the question whether human society is fundamentally about survival, or about the generation of "meaning" either at the individual or collective level. Second, he asks whether human society is concerned primarily with conservation or expenditure. The first question is aimed at inter-rogating naïve notions of "primitive" *and* "advanced" societies as being fundamentally about survival (and the accompanying grand narrative of progression from survival to "higher" things); the second question leads to the radical, Nietzschean rejection of conservation or "instincts of preservation", thus opposing the *economic principle* of conservation and accumulation (1998b: 44). Nietzsche theorizes the will to power as having preservation as a mere side effect; Baudrillard takes the achieve-ment of the "something more" in the will to power and argues that the "essential element" in life is precisely this "something more", beyond the moralizing "necessities" of life. Two examples are expenditure and appropriation, the latter being explained first with reference to the Soviet dacha or country house. The Soviet worker or administrator was provided with all his or her basic needs, including an apartment near the place of work, but the dacha is still coveted as something beyond everyday necessity, something with prestige and symbolic value (1998b: 45). As an aside, Baudrillard mentions that "automobiles" func-tion in a similar way in the West; without realizing it, this example combines neatly expenditure and appropriation, since an expensive top-of-the-range car has prestige and symbolic value, but it is also a wasteful expenditure given the instant, massive depreciation as soon as the vehicle is possessed (this isn't quite the same with "antique" or "classic" cars, which belong to the realm of the collectible object as theorized in *The System of Objects*). By going beyond the everyday neces-sities to define the social prestige and symbolic value of a possession, Baudrillard also sets up the structural model for affluence and waste. Affluence is not defined by there being "enough" of some object, but by there being too much, beyond the level of utility (1998b: 45). Waste, rather than being some kind of useless or dangerous by-product of the capitalist system, is seen instead as defining it: "It is that wastage which defies scarcity and, contradictorily, signifies abundance. It is not utility, but that wastage which, in its essence, lays down the psychological, sociological and economic guidelines for affluence" (1998b: 45). Unlike the symbolic value generated by the prestige enhancement of the potlatch, Western expenditure is geared up primarily to stimulating mass consumption (1998b: 46).

THE HYPERMARKET

In his *Critique of Everyday Life*, Henri Lefebvre attacks the "masses" for a lack of imagination when it comes to thinking of the future (and even, in the first place, the possibility of change), and he attacks "writers" for perceiving the future in terms of elitist pleasures. Lefebvre asks how many of these writers have theorized the future in terms of science and technology applied to the mundane, the everyday? And what such a future would look like stripped of abstract ideals in aesthetics, knowledge and power? He does, however, provide a warning:

> But should we in turn wish to "look into the future" and form an image of what it will be, there is one childish error we must avoid: to base the man of the future on what we are now, simply granting him a greater quantity of mechanical means and appliances.
>
> (Lefebvre, 1991: 246)

Much of Baudrillard's work seems to be predicting the future, hovering on the edge or divide between the present and fantastic (and at times absurd) possibilities. But closer analysis of Baudrillard's work shows that he is often simply mapping (and, of course, interpreting) the most contemporary manifestation of human behaviour in the West: ultimately, he is an anthropologist working within his own society who is aware of the need to examine the qualitative changes rather than the mere quantitative. Consequently, the issue of where and how we buy or consume our technological objects is as important as what those objects do (be they gadgets, gizmos or robots): the "hypermarket" (or "out-of-town" shopping centre) is a place that has gone beyond the commodity, beyond the traditional spaces of representation and consumption, even beyond the sign. In the hypermarket, the technological and other objects become hypercommodities.

Baudrillard calls the hypermarkets "triage centres" (1994a: 75); that is to say, places where people are tested and sorted according to preprogrammed categories. The hypermarket may be modelled on a traditional downtown or centre-of-town street market or shopping area, but this is just a surface effect or myth, a way of making people feel that they are getting some kind of authentic experience in a sanitized, safer environment. The modern shopping area was centralized, placed to use a clichéd phrase in the *heart* of the urban community. The hypermarket is decentred, a satellite that creates a gravitational pull on the suburbs, constructing spatial and temporal distortions that harden into new patterns of behaviour analogous to the rhythms of commuting. It would be a mistake to situate the hypermarket at the end of a social and architectural chain, an effect of new modes of living and consuming; instead, and especially in the US as Baudrillard notes, the hypermarket is responsible for "the metro area"; that is, a place which is neither country nor city, neither purely rural or purely urbanized. The "metro area" is itself decentred, projected and anticipated by its model: the hypermarket. In this sense the hypermarket isn't simply postmodern because of its decentred nature, but because it is a model generating new geographical and experiential space (see Chapter 5). And, if the hypermarket is hyperreal, the metaphor which describes it is based upon the television screen: consumers who pass through this space are "screened" or tested. Do they respond to the preprogramming as they are supposed to? The objects in the hypermarket are not there simply to be consumed, or interpreted as signs of something else (say, "affluence"), but instead they are described by Baudrillard as "tests". In other words, the consumer comes to the hypermarket with his or her anxieties and questions, and hopes to find them answered in the objects. The deliberate vagueness here is indicative of Baudrillard's theoretical approach when it comes to mapping out contemporary human behaviour as an anthropologist, but what he is actually describing is the hypermarket as a replacement for the organized religion of Western society. The circularity of the "screening" or "testing" during this experience derives from the way in which these concepts are based upon televisual feedback: the audience responses and media referenda that generate "answers" along the lines of preprogrammed "questions". And there is an interpenetration of the screen metaphor with the notion of everything being on the surface here, including the "friendly" surveillance which simultaneously shows the people under surveillance on television screens, which leads to a collapsing of perspectival space (the removal of the "gap" or distance both spatially and temporally between the viewer and the viewed). The interpenetration is total, including architectural and geographical space: "The hypermarket cannot be separated from the highways that surround and feed it, from the parking lots blanketed in automobiles, from the computer terminal – further still in concentric circles – from the whole town as a total functional screen of activities" (1994a: 76).

Unlike the modernist factory, where the workers were isolated and fixed in one spot as the product they were working on was brought to/past them, here the workers have been set free; their behaviour is now playful in the sense that their time and motion appears spent according to whim or other unknown factors. But the model of the hypermarket prevails: everything is neatly laid out for the workers, just as everything they need to produce is available to them at all times (computer terminals). The model may have changed – modern factory and centred city to postmodern computer terminal and decentred metro area – but the apparent freedoms are still "disciplines", which may have less choice involved than it first appears.

The city can no longer absorb this new space of being – the city as we have seen is transformed by the satellite into a metropolitan area. Strictly functional urban zones, categorized as commerce, work, knowledge and leisure, are not only displaced and deterritorialized, but they are also made indeterminate, with a blurring of "functional" boundaries. Baudrillard thus calls the hypermarket and all its analogous manifestations "negative satellites" (1994a: 78). The indeterminate functioning of satellitic space is analogous to the nuclear power station: a series of boxes which have no apparent function but still have an input/output, like a logic gate in a microprocessor.

SUMMARY

One of the key components of postmodernism is technology. In this chapter we have seen how Baudrillard was analysing technology from his earliest publication in 1968. However, *The System of Objects* also prefigures the later postmodern work, exploring themes that are embedded in his analyses of the emerging consumer society in France. Baudrillard meditates upon the way that technology has rapidly become non-functional, non-utilitarian, and designed according to fantasy and desire. Automatism dominates the technological object, as well as new notions of "fuzzy" logic or indeterminacy. Objects become "gizmos" which represent fetishism and fashion. Hypermarkets become the new experiential spaces of technology and consumption, the spaces of everyday life.

3

NARRATIVES OF PRIMITIVISM

The "last real book"

In Baudrillard's early more political and "sociological" writings, there are numerous references to "primitive" societies and anthropological accounts of indigenous peoples. One of Baudrillard's key concepts – that of "symbolic exchange" – is drawn from these accounts of so-called "primitive" peoples. But who exactly are these peoples that Baudrillard refers to? And how accurate is his use of anthropological terms such as the "potlatch"? This chapter examines Baudrillard's own warning that "Alluding to primitive societies is undoubtedly dangerous ..." in relation to the fact that such allusions permeate virtually all of Baudrillard's writings.

THE TASADAY

Two narratives of "decay through exposure" fascinate Baudrillard in *Simulacra and Simulation* (1981; English edition 1994a): the Tasaday and Ramses II. In 1971, the Philippine government returned to the jungle the indigenous "lost tribe" of the Tasaday people, who were "disintegrating" upon their recent contact with the contemporary world. An analogy is then constructed by Baudrillard with the decay of Ramses (the mummified remains of the King of Egypt who died in 1225 BC), rotting in a Western museum after having survived the previous forty centuries. What Baudrillard doesn't make clear is that the Tasaday were probably part of an elaborate hoax devised to manipulate genuine indigenous peoples and control land. Both the Tasaday and Ramses decay upon coming into "visual contact" with Western society, although for Baudrillard, we are all now "living specimens" who come under the "spectral light of ethnology" (1994a: 8). Bringing into view is necessary for our society, one which is based upon production and continual gain; we must see the past not only to believe in it but to compare and contrast our achievements with it (which means our superior distance *from* it). Baudrillard then sets up another analogy: with the "Renaissance Christians" fascinated by the "American Indians" who had never been taught the doctrines of Christianity:

> Thus, at the beginning of colonization, there was a moment of stupor and bewilderment before the very possibility of escaping the universal law of the Gospel. There were two possible responses: either admit that this Law was not universal, or exterminate the Indians to efface the evidence.
>
> (1994a: 10)

Discovery or conversion of these indigenous peoples is the same thing as cultural extermination (although narratives of the loss or decline of indigenous peoples are often highly suspect in terms of the romanticization and misinterpretation that they represent). Cultural extermination can result from "museumification" (Baudrillard's play on the word "mummification") or "demuseumification" (1994a: 10–11). In the former, the indigenous subject/artefact is removed from its cultural context and destroyed by being put on display (exposed to the destructive light of contemporary culture); in the latter, the "return" of the subject/artefact to its "original" context is an attempt to recover authenticity and reality through the construction of a simulation. The Tasaday are not returned untouched to their "original" locale; instead they are placed in the equivalent of a purified theme park or "safari" park, where no visitors may go. No matter how isolated from the modern world, it is still an artificial space which encloses and protects contemporary notions of the primitive – what the primitive should be, how it should exist, how it should function. And, as we will see from the example of Disneyland, the theme park exists to hide the fact that the "outside" world is of the same order: thus we are all anthropological subjects now.

These are some of the lessons that Baudrillard wants us to learn from this section of *Simulacra and Simulation*. But what seems lacking in this section is a self-reflective awareness of the role of the indigenous "primitive" subject/society in Baudrillard's work as a whole, especially in relation to the sense that many readers have that Baudrillard's work itself functions as an artificial space protecting at times relatively untheorized notions of "primitive" peoples. The "primitive" societies represented in this text all belong to different historical periods and geographical locations; all share the same lack of contextualization by Baudrillard; and all throw up a whole host of further complicated issues concerning their representation. Baudrillard may be using each of these heterogeneous societies to stand in for Western notions of "the primitive", but if we place this use in the wider context of Baudrillard's writings we must start questioning the replication at times of the processes criticized here. Another way of thinking about this use of "primitive" peoples is to examine Ludwig Wittgenstein's (1889–1951) "Remarks on Frazer's *Golden Bough*". Wittgenstein asserts that Frazer's "...explanations of primitive practices are much cruder than the meaning of these practices themselves" (1993: 131). Baudrillard argues a similar point when it comes to Marxism's view of "primitive" peoples and, in the above extract from *Simulacra and Simulation*, he suggests that ethnologists are blind to the ultimate effects of their otherwise "sensitive" advice. Wittgenstein suggested that it was wrong to work from a position of perceived "error" in "primitive" rites and then offer pseudoscientific explanations of those error-ridden ways; invariably, this leads to a notion of temporal development or progression, "showing" (which really means "interpreting") a people coming to gradual enlightenment. Instead, a "primitive" system should be sketched out and left to function in its own right:

> The historical explanation, the explanation as an hypothesis of development, is only *one* way of assembling the data of their synopsis. It is just as possible to see the data in their relation to one another and to embrace them in a general picture without putting it in the form of a hypothesis about temporal development.
>
> (Wittgenstein 1993: 131)

Following this almost to the letter, Baudrillard opposes a "general picture" of *symbolic exchange* to many facets of contemporary society. But before analysing his notion of "primitive" peoples, it is necessary to sketch out this "general picture".

SYMBOLIC EXCHANGE

Opposed to contemporary society in virtually all of its manifestations, symbolic exchange is a process whereby the status of the individuals involved changes as much as the status of the object. Baudrillard argues that the gift is the example of symbolic exchange closest to us as moderns/postmoderns: with the act of giving, the object loses its "objectness" and becomes instead part of the relations of exchange or, "...the transferential pact that it seals between two persons ..." (1981: 64). The object given doesn't partake of an economy of use-value (the gift itself may be utterly "useless") or exchange-value (the gift isn't a commodity or an abstract expression of its mode of production and circulation – see Chapter 4). The object given does, however, acquire symbolic exchange-value. From where does Baudrillard draw this notion of symbolic exchange? On which "primitive" societies does he base his grand narrative? And what concrete examples does he give us to understand his argument? The two main textual sources are particularly interconnected: Marcel Mauss's *The Gift* (1925; English edition 1990) and Georges Bataille's "The Notion of Expenditure" (1933; English edition). Both of these texts draw, above all, on the notion of the "potlatch" in "primitive" societies.

BATAILLE'S POTLATCH

Bataille takes a particular strand of "gift giving" from Mauss's book, and concentrates on the notion that gift giving is opposed to crude Western theories of "barter"; in other words, rather than having some fantasy narrative of "primitives" working their way to civilization from bartering economies through to early forms of money and credit, gift giving exists as a self-contained system outside of capitalism. Bataille notes that:

> ...the archaic form of exchange has been identified by Mauss under the name *potlatch*, borrowed from the Northwestern American Indians who provided such a remarkable example of it. Institutions analogous to the Indian *potlatch*, or their traces, have been very widely found.
>
> (1985: 121)

This statement, which seems so innocent, contains a number of issues that can help with the analysis of Baudrillard's use of "primitive" peoples. For a start, the actual name *potlatch* is claimed to have been "borrowed" temporarily by Mauss (he will presumably, at some stage, give it back). Mauss is thus himself implicated in the logic of the potlatch structure from the start – but this point will be returned to. Who has lent Mauss the *potlatch*? The answer is the "Northwestern American Indians". Who are these people? Bataille lists Tlingit, Haida, Tsimshian and Kwakiutl. Unlike Mauss, Bataille makes no attempt to locate these groups in the colonial worlds of Alaska and British Columbia (or America and Canada). Neither does he trace the history of *the word that has been borrowed* – the history of the word "potlatch". However, Bataille does provide some narrative detail:

> The least advanced of these American tribes practice *potlatch* on the occasion of a person's change in situation – initiations, marriages, funerals – and, even in a more evolved form, it can never be separated from a festival; whether it provides the occasion for this festival, or whether it takes place on the festival's occasion. *Potlatch* excludes all bargaining and, in general, it is constituted by a considerable gift of riches, offered openly and with the goal of humiliating, defying, and *obligating* a rival. The exchange value of the gift results from the fact that the donee, in order to efface the humiliation and respond to the challenge, must satisfy the obligation ... to respond later with a more valuable gift, in other words, to return with interest.
>
> (1985: 121)

Bataille goes on to discuss the spectacular destruction of wealth, which is of great interest for his own writings on excessive behaviour and transgression. He also discusses the way in which status or "rank" arises in potlatching societies from the loss or partial destruction of property (1985: 122). Thus, when gifts of great value are given away at a potlatch or even destroyed, the giver gains in other forms of prestige. Apart from one more brief reference to the Kwakiutl totem poles, the potlatch in this account becomes a concept that can be used to analyse class in contemporary society:

> As Bataille understands it, gift giving does not mark a limit between civilization and barbarity. Rather, it is the demise of the potlatch, the loss of the practice of

loss, that signifies the transition from a society dominated by an aristocracy to an industrial society dominated by a bourgeoisie.

(Bracken, 1997: 45)

In other words, the bourgeoisie efface and interiorize their consumption of wealth; public displays of consumption are measured and mediocre, losing their efficacy. Worse still, the obligation publicly to expend wealth (or redistribute wealth) is refused, leading to a mean and hypocritical ruling class. Bataille argues that the explosion of class struggle is a direct manifestation of this loss of sumptuary excess and expenditure; in other words, class struggle maintains the principle of excessive *social* expenditure. The bourgeoisie, unlike the potlatching societies, theoretically negate the differences between wealthy and poor, master and slave, with their homogenizing, rationalizing society. But the homogenization is a myth revealed as such on a daily basis as the masters separate themselves from the "slaves" or workers. In other words, the masters and the workers may both share a work ethic, but the aim of the latter is survival, while the aim of the former is to separate themselves from the workers. Using a rather watered-down version of Hegel's master/slave narrative, Bataille argues that the improvement of the workers' conditions is a failure truly to separate masters and workers in an excessive display of expenditure/destruction. This leads to a reduction in the stature and pleasure of the master until, under a general state of apathy, the whole system can only move forwards again with a spectacular uprising of the workers. Class struggle can thus be interpreted as having the symbolic weight of exchange in potlatching societies. Perhaps it is via this reading of Bataille that a passage from Baudrillard referred to in Chapter 1 (see p. 22), can be reconsidered. In "Requiem for the Media" (in *For a Critique of the Political Economy of the Sign*), we have seen how Baudrillard rejects the notion that the media can be reformed or revolutionized because it already partakes of an economy of the sign, where so-called "symbolic" action is reproduced with ease: the media constructs signs of revolution from a pre-existing model. Any notion of genuine communication is lost as the model already contains feedback structures, such as audience telephone polls, which present a façade of audience interaction. Underneath this façade is the fact that the outcome of an event is constructed in advance – for example, the "natural" cycles of a strike, leading to a number of possible resolutions or permutations, instead of a strike escalating to the point where a new type of society is born. As noted in Chapter 1 (see p. 23), Baudrillard argues for a "real" media in the May 1968 uprising:

> The real revolutionary media during May were the walls and their speech, the silk-screen posters and the hand-painted notices, the street where speech began and was exchanged – everything that was an *immediate* inscription, given and returned, spoken and answered, mobile in the same space and time, reciprocal and antagonistic.
>
> (1981: 176)

Re-reading this passage in the light of Bataille's comments on the potlatch, and class struggle as being the contemporary manifestation of sumptuary expenditure, we can see that speech itself gains symbolic weight from the processes of exchange. This passage from Baudrillard is less a nostalgia trip, as asserted by critic Steven Connor (1989: 50–62), and more a reference to a recovery of symbolic exchange in contemporary society. The inscriptions consumed on the streets of Paris involved a proximity and immersion in the site of resistance, analogous at some level to the proximity and immersion of the participants in a potlatch. But even in this analogy we must demarcate the sources of the word "potlatch", noting that the analogy can only be constructed by combining Bataille's potlatch and Baudrillard's symbolic exchange. Does Baudrillard's other key source – Mauss's *The Gift* – enable us to map out the word/concept "potlatch" in any more detail?

MAUSS'S POTLATCH

After Bataille's minimalist account of the potlatch, Mauss's account provides the reader with an embarrassment of riches or detail. In examining a type of gift giving that constructs a system of total services, Mauss decides to use one word to summarize or account for these "total services":

> We propose to call this form "potlatch", as moreover, do American authors using the Chinook term, which has become part of the everyday language of

> Whites and Indians from Vancouver to Alaska. The word potlatch essentially means "to feed", "to consume".
>
> (1990: 6)

Mauss hints at the instability or indeterminacy of this word "potlatch" in two footnotes, the first a footnote to his introduction, where he says:

> ... it does not seem to us that the meaning propounded [by early accounts?] is the original one. In fact Boas gives the word potlatch – in Kwakiutl, it is true, and not in Chinook – the meaning of "feeder", and literally, "place of being satiated ..."
>
> (1990: 86, fn. 13)

In a later footnote Mauss notes that

> ... it seems that neither the idea nor the nomenclature behind the use of this term have in the languages of the Northwest the kind of preciseness that is afforded them in the Anglo-Indian "pidgin" that has Chinook as its basis.
>
> (1990: 122, fn. 209)

Baudrillard, through Bataille, through Mauss, will use a term as the absolute other to contemporary manifestations of Western society, when the term itself is highly dubious, unstable and indeterminate. In *The Potlatch Papers* (1997), Chris Bracken traces this indeterminacy with great skill, noting that it was in Canada in 1873 that William Spragge used the term *"Patlatches"*, derived from Israel Wood Powell, the "Indian superintendent" in Victoria, British Columbia, who generated reports for the year 1872. There is a problem with *what* the word describes right from the start. Did the word describe acts of pure gift giving, in effect a destruction of property since there is no return, or did the word describe an economy of exchange, where gifts are returned at a later date? Bracken notes:

> In the discourse on "Indian Affairs" the difficulty of deciding whether these practices involve gift giving or exchange is supplemented by the difficulty of naming them. Though Powell calls them "Patlatches" in 1872, an undecidability never ceases to haunt this word as it circulates through government dispatches.
>
> (1997: 36–37)

Mauss borrowed this word "potlatch", but even Mauss isn't sure, like the Canadian government, from whom the word has been borrowed. Mauss calls the word "potlatch" "precise" (1990: 122), whereas the actual Native words that *seem* to be describing facets of potlatching are "numerous, varying, and concrete ..." and, worse still, overlap in terms of their meanings (1990: 123). Mauss is setting up a binary opposition between a European-influenced language – "...the Anglo-Indian 'pidgin' that has Chinook as its basis" (1990: 122) – and the Native languages or "...archaic nomenclature" (1990: 123). This binary opposition functions along the lines of European languages = conceptual preciseness and conceptuality, Native languages = conceptual indeterminacy or vagueness and "concreteness". In other words, European languages can theorize and philosophize, whereas Native languages directly represent the naming of concrete objects or things, or processes that involve those objects or things. A trading language – the pidgin "Chinook" – becomes more advanced conceptually than an indigenous language. Mauss has thus neatly sidestepped his worries about the indeterminacy of the word "potlatch" by deciding that it is a conceptual word that is more accurate in terms of the abstracted processes of potlatching than the cultures and languages from which this abstraction is in part derived. Conveniently, the entire history of colonial interventions and appropriations is left out of the account of the potlatch, even though the word itself derives from the economic and political concerns of a colonial power.

DANGEROUS NARRATIVES OF PRIMITIVISM

In chapter 1 of *For a Critique of the Political Economy of the Sign*, Baudrillard gives a warning – whether announced in general or more specifically to himself is not clear – but the warning is unequivocal: "Alluding to primitive societies is undoubtedly dangerous ..." (1981: 30). This warning appears early on in Baudrillard's career, and then seems to be ignored, with the myriad references to "primitive" societies that follow. How are we to interpret this warning in light of Baudrillard's continual transgression of it? Did he simply decide that he was wrong? What does the warning mean? Where precisely does the danger lie? Does the danger lie in the incorrect or misrepresentative use of so-called "primitive societies"? Or is the danger something far wider-reaching, meaning that alluding to "primitive societies" can eventually destabilize the categories of Western thought? Immediately after giving the warning, Baudrillard launches into an analysis of the "original" consumption of goods and the way in which this consumption was based not upon needs, but from "cultural constraint" (1981: 30). In other words, the process of consumption is an institution that registers and reinforces social hierarchy. Apart from the dubiousness of the notion of the *original* consumption, Baudrillard does launch into a narrative of "primitive" behaviour to contextualize his use of these concepts. He refers to the Trobriand Islanders and their division between the circulation or "consumption" of classes of objects, called the *Kula* and the *Gimwali*. The Kula is a symbolic exchange and the Gimwali a commercial exchange. Baudrillard argues that this division between symbolic and commercial has all but disappeared in contemporary society, in favour of the dominance of the latter, but the principle of the Kula remains in place because

> ...behind all the superstructures of purchase, market, and private property, there is always the mechanism of social prestation which must be recognized in our choice, our accumulation, our manipulation and our consumption of objects.

(1981: 30)

A "sociological theory of objects" will thus be based upon the principle of the Kula/potlatch replacing the importance of use-value with symbolic exchange-value. In this section Baudrillard really does "allude" to "primitive" societies, giving us the bare-bones structure of the Trobriand Islanders and using the word "potlatch" twice: once in the title of the section (*Symbolic Exchange: the "Kula'" and the "Potlatch"*), and once in the text (*Potlatch*). The allusion to the potlatch with no accompanying description may depend upon the reader having read the anthropologists Bronislaw Kasper Malinowski (1884–1942) and Marcel Mauss on the Trobriand Islanders (Baudrillard does cite Malinowski by name as a source); in which case, as Mauss argues, the Kula is not actually different from the potlatch: "The *Kula* is a sort of grand potlatch" (1990: 21). But, if the reader knows this, and agrees with this point or conflation (not forgetting that potlatch is a precise concept not a concrete "naming" word), then why does Baudrillard feel the need to keep "*Kula*" and "*Potlatch*" separate as words in the first place? Perhaps Baudrillard's allusion to the potlatch is dangerous because it signifies not just a concept that he is going to use to critique Marxism, but it also signifies that his allusion itself reveals a more complex and potentially destabilizing world beneath or behind the concept of potlatch. Bracken notes how the early use of "potlatch" was itself contained in quote marks and parentheses, the use of which "...suggests, if inadvertently, that here 'potlatches' is itself a problem in need of a solution and does not refer to an event" (1997: 39). Further, what is found "...on the west coast of Vancouver Island ... is not a word that asks to be discussed but a practice that Western civilization wants above all to exclude from itself: the practice of non-productive expenditure ..." (1997: 39). Baudrillard seems to be saying that the conflation of Kula and potlatch is dangerous because it is in their speci- ficity as exchange events that their power as abstracted concepts resides, yet it is the conflation, and thus removal, of their specificity which activates them as concepts for Western readers or theorists. "Potlatch" is therefore functioning at this early stage in Baudrillard's work as another deconstructive term, or something used to interrogate Western philosophical systems of thought. The work of deconstruction at this point overrides necessarily (although still problematically) the accuracy of his use of non-Western societies and concepts. But is this the case throughout Baudrillard's work? Is it the potlatch only which functions as a deconstructive term?

DECONSTRUCTION

The term "deconstruction" is widely attributed to its most famous propo- nent, Jacques Derrida (1930–), who is known mainly for three early books, all published in French in 1967: *Speech and Phenomena* (1973), *Of Grammatology* (1976) and *Writing and Difference* (1978). However, an earlier use of the word "deconstruction" can be found in the related work of philosopher Martin Heidegger (1889–1976), who in his main book *Being and Time* discusses the notion of a "critical dismantling". The latter defini- tion is generally the one used, unreflectively, by literary and cultural critics. Indeed, it is necessary to distinguish between a philosophical and non-philosophical notion of deconstruction because these positions can vary quite considerably.

"PHILOSOPHICAL" DECONSTRUCTION

Derrida's project of exploring the limits of metaphysics (systems of thought that articulate grand concepts such as "truth" and "being") is achieved via the use of a number of philosophical tools. Derrida examines the founding binary oppositions of metaphysics and argues that the excluded side of each binary opposition is actually implicit within metaphysics all along. Therefore, metaphysical arguments must contain blind spots or "aporias" where certain excluded binaries cannot be seen or accounted for by those same arguments. Deconstructive tools are built from these unaccountable binaries, and include neologisms or new words and phrases, that can be used to explore metaphysical reasoning from within. For example, Derrida argues that the "supplement", something which is both an addition and a substitute, works via a deconstructive logic. Philosophers have argued that writing is both something unnecessary, if not damaging, to original speech (a substitution), yet also supplementary – that is to say, needed to fulfil original speech (an addition). In other words, one of the founding binary oppositions of metaphysics, that of the priority of speech over writing, or the "live" voice over the "dead" letter, is called into question by the supplement as deconstructive tool.

"NON-PHILOSOPHICAL" DECONSTRUCTION

Literary and cultural thinkers have created a critical approach called deconstruction, drawing upon key Derridean ideas and terms, without necessarily understanding or "importing" the philosophical contexts and purposes of those terms. This can lead to a debased parody of Derrida's project. Nonetheless, such a non-philosophical approach is arguably the most popular and most widespread way of understanding deconstruction. The popular approach takes "dismantling" literally, and regards deconstruction as a breaking apart of oppressive systems, then going on to rebuild the systems with a new set of values. Clearly such an approach is useful to other types of criticism, such as feminism and postcolonialism, if only as a first move in a larger theoretical argument or process, whereby a philosophical rigour is returned to. This can lead to hybrid forms of criticism, which contain a deconstructive component. Popular deconstruction focuses on the hierarchies implicit in systems built upon binary oppositions (e.g. good/bad, male/female), and normally aims at a reversal of them. Philosophical deconstruction argues that the reversal is a temporary, strategic move that doesn't really take us "outside" of metaphysics, because the hierarchical system has merely been reorganized (hierarchy is still in place). Popular deconstruction regards this reversal as far more radical and liberating, going beyond closed, formal systems. While popular deconstruction has largely been absorbed into the general background of literary and cultural theory, or simply been rejected outright (having reached its peak in the raging theoretical debates of the 1980s), it is arguable that the questions raised by philosophical deconstruction are still of value and interest.

In *Symbolic Exchange and Death*, the narratives of "primitivism", from a postcolonial perspective, take on a regressive form: non-Western peoples have become unspecified "savages". Chapter 5 opens with a sweeping statement which, while part of the theoretical argument under construction, isn't given any cultural specificity: "As soon as savages began to call 'men' only those who were members of their tribe, the definition of the 'Human' was considerably enlarged" (1998a: 125).

POSTCOLONIALISM

A term used most widely to theorize the ongoing impact that colonialism has upon people in the modern world. For example, British Columbia's First Nations are only just beginning to get properly negotiated treaties with the Provincial and Canadian governments. In other words, many years after Britain's colonial presence in Canada was withdrawn, it is still affecting indigenous people's lives. Gilbert and Tompkins argue that postcolonialism is "...an engagement with and contestation of colonialism's discourses, power structures, and social hierarchies" (1996: 2). Postcolonialism is often studied in a variety of academic subject areas, such as cultural studies, literature and sociology.

Baudrillard does refer to Jean de Léry's sixteenth-century *Histoire d'un voyage en la terre de Brésil*, but there is no sense of an empirical or anthropological basis to the use of the word "savages". Baudrillard is utilizing the Western discourse of "primitivism", whereby generic "savages" live in generic "tribes", supposedly existing utterly outside of the West, although in reality they live nowhere but in the West's psyche. The problematic status of this generic existence in conceptual material is illustrated neatly by Wittgenstein in his "Remarks on Frazer's *Golden Bough*". Wittgenstein argues that "Frazer is much more savage than most of his savages, for they are not as far removed from the understanding of a spiritual matter as a twentieth-century Englishman" (1993: 131). While this is an explicit critique of Frazer and his comprehension of the Other, the problem lies in the reversal of the civilized/savage binary opposition. To say that Frazer is more "savage" than a "savage" is merely to reverse the binary opposition and simultaneously keep its values in place. In other words, non-Western cultures may have complex societies that Wittgenstein thinks people like Frazer cannot grasp in all their complexities, but they are still societies fundamentally inferior to Western civilization. The tying in of the two uses of the word "savage" also undermines the reversal that Wittgenstein attempts to articulate; Frazer's "savage" nature necessarily contaminates the generic use of the noun "savage/s". This is an important point in relation to Baudrillard's use of narratives of primitivism: if he is always presenting the "savages" as an absolute Other to the West, then he has simply performed a reversal of values. If, on the other hand, he can prove that the concepts of "savage", "primitive" or "potlatch", for example, are aporias – blind spots that unravel the founding presuppositions of Western thought – then his primitivist discourse is deconstructive in some sense. But, this primitivist discourse may be operating to deconstruct Baudrillard's work as much as he is trying to do the same to the "non-symbolic".

Baudrillard expands his thus far rather limited account of "primitives" in the chapter "Political Economy and Death" in his *Symbolic Exchange and Death*, with a number of narratives: initiation ceremonies, incest prohibition and cannibalism. Overall, *Symbolic Exchange and Death* is about the way in which in contemporary society the symbolic is replaced by the semiotic. Contemporary society turns all objects into commodities, which circulate endlessly like signs: thus objects lose the inherent value that they "once" had, and the types of value gained in processes such as the potlatch, for example, in the gift of a hand-woven blanket. *Symbolic Exchange and Death* also asserts that the concept of death must now be set outside of society, denied, effaced, repressed, and so on, instead of being an integral part of a society's beliefs. Rex Butler argues that in many respects this book is "...in part a history and sociology of the place of death in Western society" (1999: 98):

> from the dead time or labour implied in the modern industrial process in the chapter "The End of Production" (*SE*, 6–50), through the self-punishment and discipline required in the new regime of health and fitness in the chapter "The Body, or the Grave of Signs" (*SE*, 101–124), and on to the actual suppression or hiding of death in the funeral parlour or retirement home in the chapter "Political Economy and Death" (*SE*, 125–195).
>
> (Butler, 1999: 98)

How does Baudrillard's use of "primitives" help his argument? In other words, how does the reference to "primitives" prove that there was a state of affairs prior to the semiotic? Baudrillard argues that, for "primitives", death is a social relation and that, paradoxically, death is a more material fact for such people because they are aware of and function with the form of death. In contrast, Western societies conceive of death as a biological fact or materiality, whereby the dead are separated utterly from the living: *the dead cease to exist*. Baudrillard argues that initiation rites are one way in which death as a social relation is articulated. In Christian societies, the subject has his or her mortality emphasized by the ritual of baptism; in "primitive" societies, the biological birth similarly does not lead to socialization, and requires a ritualized supplement. In the latter case it is the initiation ceremony that is a symbolic birth/death:

> The important moment is when the *moh* (the grand priests) put the *koy* (the initiates) to death, so that the latter are then consumed by their ancestors, then the earth gives birth to them as their mother had given birth to them. After having been "killed", the initiates are left in the hands of their initiatory, "cultural" parents, who instruct them, care for them and train them (initiatory birth).
>
> (1998a: 131–132)

A material, irreversible death has been replaced by one that has been given and received. Death is a gift, as well as birth; no longer the monocultural mortality of "giving birth", but instead the multivalent giving birth/giving death. Initiation is theorized as a doubling of birth/death through symbolic exchange, not to "outdo" or "eclipse" death, but to remove the division of birth from death, the splitting or disjunction which contemporary society uses to efface death. Baudrillard argues that Western society functions via a disjunctive code, where the real is generated through the "...structural effect of the disjunction between two terms ..." (1998a: 133). This will be more familiar in relation to the binary oppositions that society structures itself through, where one side of the binary is prioritized according to the prevailing ideology, e.g. male/female, white/black, and so on. Baudrillard argues that the symbolic does not allow for the operation of this binary disjunction. This is because Baudrillard regards the symbolic as something that is not a structure, but an act or process that "heals" divisions within society. Problematically, this can lead to idealized and romanticized accounts of "primitive" peoples living totally "in touch" with nature, and so on. While Baudrillard doesn't use these images as such, the logic of his argument leads inexorably in this direction.

Where are the "primitive" peoples Baudrillard uses in his discussion of initiation ceremonies, incest prohibition and cannibalism? With references to anthropological accounts by writers such as Maurice Leenhardt, Jean de Léry and Marcel Mauss among others, the reader is given an abstracted "savage" or "primitive" race that is an amalgam of all these accounts. The discussion on cannibalism, for example, locates this practice not in ancient times, but among a Catholic rugby team whose aeroplane crashed, as Baudrillard narrates, into the Cordillera in the Andes (1998a: 137). Baudrillard's point is that cannibalism is in itself a symbolic act, not some "savage" giving-into transgressive desire; devouring is a mark of exchange not a consumption of "vital forces", in that it creates a respectful relationship with the dead, who are being paid homage to. What is important in this account, again, is the *location* of this devouring: "In any case they don't just eat anybody, as we know ..." (1998a: 138). "We" are given no further information about the "they" in this sentence, at the same time as "we" are awarded knowledge of the "they". Logically, the "they" are the cannibals, the subject of this section, but the only cannibals that have been located for us are the Catholic rugby team! The sequence: "primitives" = "cannibals" = "the 'they'" has been interrupted and crossed over, whereby we get something like: "primitives" = "cannibals" = "Catholic rugby team". This crossover would seem to suggest that the absolute Other has always been the same, and that the same has always been the absolute Other. Put another way, Baudrillard is trying to oppose Western society with something drawn from its own conceptual and ideological framework. In answer to the question "Where are the 'primitive' peoples?", the answer must be: They have vanished, or they were never there in the first place. And this is why Baudrillard's continual reference to "primitive" societies must be closely examined and watched out for at all times: when he claims to be looking at "primitive" societies, he is often only articulating Western myths and structures concerning the Other. He claims to access something radically different from the West, when his statements on "primitive" societies are based firmly upon the West.

Critics have discussed *Symbolic Exchange and Death* as Baudrillard's last "real" book, with virtually everything produced afterwards suffering from a "permanent misunderstanding" (Gane, 1993: 189). In his introduction to *Jean Baudrillard: The Defence of The Real*, Butler discusses this point at length, noting that *Symbolic Exchange and Death* is regarded as:

> ... the last of Baudrillard's books that is observational, empirical, scientific. It is the last that comes out of his discipline, that could be taught in a conventional course, in sociology. Death ... is a real object, something that exists out there in the world before it is written about. It is a topic that can be measured, of which a history can be constructed, that is not simply a fabrication of Baudrillard himself. Henceforth, Baudrillard's work becomes fictional, inventive, "pataphysical".
>
> (1993: 5)

Mike Gane notes that it is in *Symbolic Exchange and Death* that Baudrillard expresses "...his argument in more orthodox terms" (1993: xiii). While the latter is undoubtedly true, the reading of Baudrillard's "primitivism" presented here undermines the notion that *Symbolic Exchange and Death* presents "observational, empirical, [and] scientific" material. One way of addressing the perceived differences between the earlier, supposedly "sociological" work and the later "performative" writing involves a simple comparison for "truth" content. *Fatal Strategies* (first published 1983; translation 1990b) contains a number of references to "primitives" and the potlatch (or

"potlach"), for example, "primitive people" share a principle of "fundamental duplicity" that allows them to both affirm and negate their
gods: "...they invented them only to put them to death, and drew their
energy from this intermittent sacrifice" (1990: 77). Baudrillard gives
this decentring drive one example – the Aztecs – and then relates
duplicity as a strategic, fatal act to Bataille. Similarly with "gaming",
which is shown to be something different from the transgressive activities of "...potlach [sic] and expenditure" as theorized by Bataille (1990:
53). "Primitives" are narrated as *having lived* with the burden of predes-
tination and an ordered universe: "Primitives believed in a world of this
kind, a world of the omnipotent thought and will, without the shadow
of a chance. But they lived really in magic and cruelty" (1990: 148).
The past tense signifies that this universal world-view was once the
case, but exists no longer. "Primitives" are doubly condemned here,
having no cultural or historical specificity and existing in the past only.
But this simulacrum of "primitives" is essentially the same as found in
the earlier "empirical" studies; in fact, by presenting "primitives"
without the narrative detail found in the earlier works, the simulacrum
is simply more obviously just that. In other words, the use of the
"potlatch" throughout Baudrillard's work is actually the use of the
"potlack" – a simulation of "primitivism" which is always lacking and
excessive at the same time. But this, paradoxically, means that to
critique Baudrillard's use of "primitives" as being inaccurate is to miss
the point that, from the very beginning, he has been working with a
simulacrum of "primitivism". This in turn leads to a destabilization of
what Baudrillard means by "the real" or an Other to contemporary
society. No longer seen as laughable nostalgia, Baudrillard's continual
reference to "archaic" cultures demands further (more serious)
analysis.

SUMMARY

The need for Westerners to "see" the past to compare it with modern society leads to an intense fascination with so-called "primitive" societies, which are visually interesting and impressive. Baudrillard continually "displays" "primitive" peoples in his work, and this chapter explores the way in which such a series of displays is highly problematic. Baudrillard's concept of symbolic exchange is examined in relation to Mauss and Bataille and, using the colonial word for such indigenous practices, the potlatch. The chapter argues that Baudrillard is using notions of "primitivism" in dubious, dangerous ways, even given his own warning against "alluding to primitive societies". Finally, the opposition between Baudrillard's early sociological writings and his later postmodern books is examined in relation to the postcolonial critique. *Symbolic Exchange and Death* has been called Baudrillard's "last real book" because it contains empirical analysis of the "real" world, examining facts and truths, whereas his postmodern books blur the boundaries between fact and fiction, analysis and performance. But, in examining the use of non-Western societies in his early work, this opposition is itself called into question.

4

REWORKING MARXISM

An important transitional phase occurs in Baudrillard's early work with his reworking of Marxism. This chapter will discuss the structuralist notions of Marxism (1968–1972) and then the strong critique of Marx from 1972 onwards. The influence of Marx within Baudrillard's work has often been overlooked in the English-speaking world. This is due in part to the fact that Baudrillard's earliest writings were mainly translated into English long after the event and because of the interest in the later more performative "postmodern" pieces. Thus, *Le Système des objets* (1968) wasn't translated until 1996, and the more Marxist books *La Société de consommation* (1970) until 1998 and *Pour une critique de l'économie politique du signe* (1972) until 1981. Only *Le Miroir de la production* (1973) was translated relatively quickly into English in 1975. The development of Marxist concepts and ideas was also downplayed by many critics because of the intense focus on postmodernism, communication theories, semiotics, and Baudrillard's relation to structuralism and poststructuralism. More serious studies of Marxism and Baudrillard arose with Kellner (1989) and Gane (1991). In this chapter we will examine the early cluster of books that are basically engaging with questions generated by Marx. In this respect, we will see that there is a definite shift of perspective with the publication of *The Mirror of Production*, whereby the attempt to construct a structural Marxism turns into something far more critical and sceptical.

STRUCTURAL MARXISM: 1968–1972

The overriding binary opposition of concern in the early Baudrillard is that of production/consumption. We can trace Baudrillard's changing relationship with or attitudes to Marxism by gauging the ways in which the key processes of production and consumption are treated. In classical Marxism – that is to say, the theory that sticks closest to Marx's original way of thinking – production is the key process in industrialized Capitalist society. In Baudrillard's early works, a strong interest in consumption is apparent, an interest arising no doubt from the application of Marxism to the modern French world of increasing wages and mass consumption of consumer goods. But Baudrillard's interest in consumption is tempered by the fact that production is still accorded priority. Why is this? Because Baudrillard had yet to engage with Marx in a critical fashion. In other words, he still believed in many of the theoretical positions as elaborated in *Das Kapital*. With *The Mirror of Production*, Baudrillard argues that contemporary French thought has become dominated by theories of production or, at the very least, the "perspective" of production in generating new ideas. So what Baudrillard says he will do is shift that perspective, from production to consumption. Therefore, to get to grips with Baudrillard's use of Marxism involves sketching out his ideas concerning consumption and then (briefly) his development of a critique of the political economy of the sign.

Baudrillard opens *The Consumer Society* with a vision of a new system of human behaviour: one of the abundant consumption of objects. Intersubjective communication is replaced with the interaction of humans, goods and whole systems that surround the manipulation of these goods. What does this mean? That instead of a world of human beings communicating at a personal one-to-one level (about daily life, political or spiritual beliefs, and so on), human beings become commodities, like consumer goods. In other words, human beings are valued for reasons other than their "humanity" and they also live their lives according to a new pattern or rhythm (a "new temporality"): that of the succession or consumption of objects. In comparison with this new temporality, Baudrillard harks back to a previous era and previous civilizations where "... it was timeless objects, instruments or monuments which outlived the generations of human beings" (1998b: 25). For example, the Christian chalice (a silver cup holding Communion wine) was an object in the past that would only ever be touched by the average person in church on a Sunday. The chalice would "outlive" the parishioners, being an object that existed in the church for centuries. In contemporary times, while this religious object is still important to many people, silver chalices are bought and sold as valuable antiques. Any person with enough money can buy a chalice one day, and sell it for profit the next. The person in this case "outlives" the object. Another related example is the cathedral, once a holy building that "outlived" the lives of the worshippers, now treated by many people within a secular society as a tourist destination, to be visited for an hour or so, and "consumed" in this way. Baudrillard argues that the jungle of objects that the subject has to negotiate on a daily basis, at home and at work, through advertisements, dreams and fantasies, are importantly the product of human activity (1998b: 26). Quoting Marx, such production is related to the law of exchange-value. In other words, there is a tension immediately made obvious by the fact that Baudrillard is mapping out the modern, contemporary world of consumerist objects, but using the more traditional logic of Marxist use and exchange-value. Marx had theorized the commodity in *Capital* as something carrying *use-value* and *exchange-value*.

USE-VALUE AND EXCHANGE-VALUE

USE-VALUE

Arises from productive activity to construct something that fulfils a need, such as shoes or clothing.

EXCHANGE-VALUE

An expression of the labour-power necessary for the production of a commodity. It is an "abstract" expression because it does not relate to the commodity itself, such as the shoes or clothes considered above, but to the cost of the labour (among other things) needed to make the commodity.

Both use- and exchange-value are anchored in production. Later on in *Capital*, Marx notes how the subject is alienated or distanced from the products of his or her own labour (in other words, the worker doesn't get to benefit from the full exchange-value of the object that he or she has produced) and the methods of production themselves, e.g. the factory machine (the worker is no longer a skilled craftsperson but a cog in that machine). For Marx, the workers' consumption is broken down into two separate entities: productive and individual consumption. Productive consumption is where the worker uses up or "consumes" his or her own energies used to make a part of something in the factory production line. But the worker passes on the benefit of the production process to the factory owner (the Capitalist). Individual consumption is the process of survival, whereby the worker uses all of his or her money to buy basic necessities such as food, shelter, clothing and heating. Individual consumption also benefits the processes of production because the workers are using all of their money to keep themselves strong enough to return to the factory the following day, whereby he or she once more expends energy which benefits the Capitalist. Marx argues: "The fact that the worker performs acts of individual consumption in his own interest, and not to please the Capitalist, is something entirely irrelevant to the matter" (1979: 718). Even while Marx is showing how individual consumption is *essentially* needed under Capitalism for the reproduction of the workforce, not the fulfilment of vicarious individual needs, he is still focusing on use-value: the worker buys a commodity to fulfil a need (and is conned in the process, but no matter, according to Capitalism). For Baudrillard, the consumption of objects by the worker is far more complex and interesting, because such consumption involves, to use critic Charles Levin's phrase, a "cultural transformation" (1996: 62). In other words, what the modern-day consumer does with the object may bear no relation to the object's use-value, but that doesn't mean that the object is not important or capable of having a profound impact upon society. Think of the personal computer hooked up to the Internet, for example, and the practice of "surfing the Web" which was initially seen by some people as a pointless activity. Now e-commerce is becoming more important and volatile, "dot.com" internet company shares are having an impact upon leading stock markets.

Baudrillard constantly asks this question: Where does this cultural transformation take place? The answer is in the everyday life of the subject, which is "the locus of consumption" (1998b: 34). Henri Lefebvre (1901–1991), in his *Critique of Everyday Life*, argued that alienation was going to be the central notion of philosophy and literature, since philosophy involved a critique of, and literature an expression of, "being in" the world (1991: 168). The fact that Marxism was beginning to dominate French thought – with the concept of alienation as another key component – meant, in other words, that "being in the world" now had to be understood via alienation. Lefebvre argued that alienation is a "fixing" of human activity in a material *and* abstract sense. What this means is that human beings in industrialized Capitalist nations no longer understand their "social relations", which were stable within older societies. Neither do human beings consider themselves as subjects given meaning by the tools they use at work – as did, according to Marxists, the craftsperson in pre-industrialized society. Now the individual is isolated, cut adrift from stable social relations, and any notion of a skilled craft or trade. It is up to the critic to penetrate the apparent relations that alienate the subject, which is to say that, while the worker cannot perceive the root cause of his or her everyday alienation, the critic can do this. Lefebvre argues: "Genuine criticism will then reveal the human reality beneath this general unreality, the human 'world' which takes shape within us and around us: in what we see and what we do, in humble objects and (apparently) humble and profound feelings" (1991: 168). Baudrillard shares with Lefebvre this notion of "unreality", but at this stage in his work he is not content with the sociological analyses of consumption that argue, crudely speaking, that the subject is conned into wanting an existence that supplies artificially constructed needs or desires via the "humble objects" of consumer society. Baudrillard builds his own idiosyncratic theories of consumption via a dovetailing of an updated critique of everyday life and Marx's theories of production.

In *The Consumer Society*, Baudrillard maps out the logic of consumption. He still argues that society is "... objectively and decisively a society of production, *an order of production* ..." but notes that the orders of production and consumption become entangled with one another (1998b: 32–33). Under the traditional Marxist analysis of alienation, consumer goods are necessarily divorced from production. For example, the (idealized) craftsperson would have constructed a given product from beginning to end, being intimately involved in all the stages of its development, from accumulating the raw materials to gaining satisfaction from seeing the finished goods. The modern worker, however, has no such relation with the product. He or she may be positioned in the factory, placing one piece of raw material in a machine over and over again, abstracting the task in its endless repetition. The product has been subsumed by the process of industrial manufacture, and the worker therefore no longer follows the construction of a particular product from beginning to end. Lefebvre argues that:

> As he strives to control nature and create his world, man conjures himself up a new nature. Certain of man's products function in relation to human reality like some impenetrable nature, undominated, oppressing his consciousness and will from without. Of course, this can only be an appearance; products of human activity cannot have the same characteristics as brute, material things. And yet this appearance too is a reality: commodities, money, capital, the State, legal, economic and political institutions, ideologies – all function as though they were realities external to man. In a sense, they are realities, with their own laws. And yet, they are purely human products ...
>
> (1991: 169)

What must be added to this equation, however, is the fact that as modern society develops there is an abundance of commodities, and an increase in wages (while Marx clearly predicted the former, he did not expect the latter to occur). The commodity may still be an entity, divorced from the mode of production, but it is not necessarily an oppressive or immediately negative thing. To explain this state of affairs, this subtle shift from alienation to increased expectation, Baudrillard constructs an analogy with the "cargo myth" of Melanesian natives, which he sees as a fable of consumer society. Baudrillard says that the Melanesian natives witnessed the descent of aeroplanes (although they had no idea what these were) to the whites, who had similar objects placed on the ground. In other words, by some apparently miraculous process, these aeroplanes brought "plenty" to the whites. However, these objects/aeroplanes never descended from the sky to the natives: the inference drawn was that the natives needed to build a simulacrum of an aeroplane to attract these objects (1998b: 31). Likewise, the modern consumer "... sets in place a whole array of sham objects, of characteristic signs of happiness, and then waits ... for happiness to alight" (1998b: 31). For example, modern-day consumers think that they will receive happiness from the object if they get themselves a new, superior model like the latest mobile phone or car. Of course, happiness does not usually arrive and, rather than the consumer interpret this as a critique of the expectation, the object is blamed: "I wouldn't feel this way if I had waited for the next, better model of mobile phone ..." and so on. Thus the waiting for happiness starts all over again. The processes of consumption are experienced therefore as magical, partly because the signs of happiness have replaced "real", total satisfaction, and because those signs are used to invoke the endlessly deferred arrival of total satisfaction: "In everyday practice, the blessings of consumption are not experienced as resulting from work or from a production process; they are experienced as a *miracle*" (1998b: 31). The miracle takes place every day on the television, which further divorces the social process of production from that of consumption, reinforcing the magical quality of the appearance and significance of the consumer object. In many respects, television "proves" the efficaciousness of the consumer object, in that it often shows people whose lives are made happier because of the expensive consumer items they possess, just as the beliefs of the Melanesians are proven by their construction of the cargo cult: that whites can live lives of plenty by diverting and capturing goods meant for the natives themselves (1998b: 32). In both instances – television and the cargo cult – a social group watch another group consuming more objects, only to confirm their belief in future abundance and happiness. Embodied in this belief is the concept of the "right" to abundance dispensed by a beneficent agency, be it technology, progress or growth (1998b: 32). But what Baudrillard is trying to suggest is that this expectation takes place via the signs of abundance, is reinforced and assuaged by the codes and symbolic systems of our societies (1998b: 33). And the latter needs the kind of investigation lacking in Marx (although he points towards such an investigation in several dense passages of *Capital*). Baudrillard regards the "universality of the news item" as characterizing consumer society because the media reduces information to a homogeneous or similar form that is both anodyne and miraculous (1998b: 33). What he means by this is that reality is both made spectacular and distant at the same time: the subject is brought seemingly closer to the world of events, but this world is consumed via signs, which keep the real at a distance. With a very early formulation that will eventually lead to notions of the hyperreal, Baudrillard argues that the media doesn't present us with reality, "... but *the dizzying whirl of reality* ..." (1998b: 34). The media appears to give us abundance when it is actually "empty" of all real content; it is the site of the playing out of our desires, protecting us at the same time from confronting the everyday realities of a dangerous and problematic world: "So we live, sheltered by signs, in the denial of the real" (1998b: 34). Such language may be shocking for those readers more familiar with the later "postmodern" writing, where notions of "reality" are problematized; but they are problematized not by the *disappearance of* the real, but by the *division from* the real. At this point in *The Consumer Society*, Baudrillard argues that he can define the practices of consumption:

> The consumer's relation to the real world, to politics, to history, to culture is not a relation of interest, investment or committed responsibility nor is it one of total indifference: it is a relation of *curiosity*. On the same pattern, we can say that the dimension of consumption as we have defined it here is not one of knowledge of the world, nor is it one of total ignorance: it is the dimension of *misrecognition*.
>
> (1998b: 34; Baudrillard's emphasis)

There are a number of unexplained issues here, such as the question of how we gain a perspective which allows the critic to see through the misrecognition and the emptiness of the curiosity, and also what a world prior to apprehension through signs was actually like. But it needs to be emphasized that such a world is clearly one prior to the alienation generated by Capitalism. In the Marxist narrative, the everyday world of the consumer is impoverished by the collusion of the media and the closed, isolated world of the private individual who attempts to find personal satisfaction in the consumption of goods – not through social relations. The world is reinterpreted according to the dictates and desires of consumption and, worse still, it is therefore subjective, unlike the objectivity of the totality (1998b: 35).

In *The Consumer Society*, Baudrillard suggests that theorists must go beyond the notion of needs as being related to specific, individual products, which are pressed upon the subject in advance of his or her purchase (or desire to purchase). For example, Baudrillard doesn't think that people are forced somehow to want a particular product, say a new car. Rather, there is a whole system of needs, which is the product of the system of production (1998b: 74). It may be difficult to distinguish the precise differences between what Baudrillard is rejecting here, and what he puts in its place. The key issue is that he wants to retain the Marxist emphasis on production, but lose the sociological reduction of consumption into a series of forced purchases based upon inflicted desires. Instead of there being some kind of one-to-one relationship between producer and consumer – say, with the producer designing and building a new type of motor car which is then projected directly to the consumer as their next desired object – there is a system of needs that is the effect of the logical progression of the system of productive forces. Baudrillard argues that the order of production doesn't seek to appropriate individual levels of enjoyment but, more radically, it denies enjoyment to supplant it with the system of needs. Thus we have a genealogy of consumption:

1   The order of production produces the machine/productive force, a technical system radically different from the traditional tool.
2   It produces capital/rationalized productive force, a rational system of investment and circulation, radically different from "wealth" and from earlier modes of exchange.
3   It produces waged labour power, an abstract, systematized productive force, radically different from concrete labour and the traditional "workmanship".
4   And so it produces needs, the *system* of needs, demand/productive force as a rationalized, integrated, controlled whole, complementary to the three others in a process of total control of the productive forces and production processes. (1998b: 75; Baudrillard's emphasis)

We can think this through in relation to the industrialized worker. First, the worker no longer understands the tools used in making a product. Before industrialization, the worker understood precisely the tools used – such as the blacksmith or the weaver. But, after industrialization, the worker became part of a "machine" (the factory) and only worked at one small part of that machine with no real comprehension of the overall unit. Baudrillard argues that this shift in the relationship between the craftsperson enjoying the fruits of his or her personal labour, and the industrialized worker alienated from the factory as machine, is the first stage in a new type of production. The second stage is non-symbolic exchange: the "product" – say a hand-crafted silver chalice, which once had spiritual significance – becomes the object valued primarily for its financial return. Thus "wealth" no longer has symbolic value or meaning (the chalice was always worth money, but that wasn't its primary significance). Instead "wealth" is now related to capital, either in the form of accumulation (savings, shares, etc.) or investment (more machines, factories, etc.). Remember that waged labour power is an abstraction, a value given to the workers' energy consumed that no longer bears any relation to the goods produced by the industrialized machine. This is the third stage that changes notions of consumption, followed by the fourth stage, the "system of needs", where consumption is not related to use-value or a further imposed desire. Rather, human beings now exist within a system of consumption where the act of buying a product is as abstract as the ways in which the products are made in the first place.

In *For a Critique of the Political Economy of the Sign*, Baudrillard calls the notion of the individual subject driven by needs to consume a real, individual object, a "… thoroughly vulgar metaphysic" (1981: 63). He suggests that analysing consumption is akin to analysing dreams in the Freudian sense: there is no point in trying to make sense of the mani- fest dream because it is a complex narrative constructed from the processes of condensation and displacement. Similarly, Baudrillard argues that merely to look at the everyday surface would be a mistake: it is the processes of an "unconscious social logic" that must be analysed in relation to the realm of everyday life (1981: 63). Baudrillard makes a number of fairly complex moves, which can be briefly summarized. First, the empirical object itself is a myth, because it is actually constructed via "… the different types of relations and significations that converge, contradict themselves, and twist around it …" (1981: 63). At this stage we can think of two categories of objects beyond the utilitarian: the collected object and the object of consumption. With the collected object, the object is imbued with personal meaning in a psychological process. Any object, from stamps to "classic" cars, can be collected – what is important is that the collector finds the act of collecting pleasurable and special. These feelings may have nothing to do with how the object functions: it doesn't matter that stamps can be put on envelopes and old cars driven. With the object of consumption, the object (say, a designer dress) has a social meaning, such as status (the wearer must have great wealth to be able to afford such a dress), prestige, fashion, and so on. But the object of consumption does not function via the utilitarian or the personal: it functions via its relations with other objects. In other words, it functions like the Saussurean sign: differentially and arbitrarily (1981: 64). Next, with the transition from pre-Capitalist societies to a Capitalist system, there is a shift from symbolic exchange to "sign-value". What does Baudrillard mean by this? In symbolic exchange, an object is given not for the sake of the object itself, but for the signification generated by the transaction (e.g. the potlatch). However, this has the strange effect of both effacing and individualizing the object, because any object will do in the process of giving (a child's drawing or a Rembrandt), yet after the gift has been received the object carries or is imbued with special meaning. (We say: "This object has sentimental value.") Under Capitalism, the object is divorced from the processes of pre-industrialized production and symbolic value and starts to function like a sign: "The sign object is neither given nor exchanged: it is appropriated, withheld and manipulated by individual subjects as a sign, that is, as coded difference. Here lies the object of consumption" (1981: 65). In other words, I might decide to wear a designer suit not to fulfil a need, but to express a difference from other people who surround me. For Baudrillard, symbolic exchange reveals concrete and transparent interpersonal relationships; with the transition to sign-value, such relationships are no longer transparent:

> The object-become-sign no longer gathers its meaning in the concrete relationship between two people. It assumes its meaning in its differential relation to other signs. Somewhat like Lévi-Strauss' myths, sign-objects exchange among themselves. Thus, only when objects are autonomized as differential signs and thereby rendered systematizable can one speak of consumption and of objects of consumption.
>
> (1981: 66)

Think of the act of wearing the designer suit again: the suit is not worn with one other person in mind, who will value the suit for its quality of workmanship, and so on. Instead, the designer suit functions or has meaning because it is not a high-street brand. The various suits function, also, regardless of who wears them (think about the fact that most catwalk models, apart from the supermodels, are anonymous people to the average consumer). In other words, designer suits circulate in the fashion world and beyond like signs – they can be worn/used by no one or anyone, and the act of wearing doesn't change what they signify. Another way of thinking about this is in relation to Saussure: wearing a suit is like the speech act or "parole". The speech act is given meaning by the system of language or "langue" overall, not the individual speaker. Thus Baudrillard's consumer indulges in acts of consumption (wearing suits), which are given meaning by the system (e.g. the fashion-system or code).

Baudrillard argues that we must distinguish, therefore, between the logic of consumption and the logic of use value, exchange-value and symbolic exchange. A clear example is that of the difference between a wedding ring and an ordinary ring. The wedding ring has symbolic value (the marriage), and in the process of being given becomes a singular object; for example, the ring isn't periodically changed for one of a different fashion, and so on. The ordinary ring, however, is not usually symbolic: it can be changed for one of a different fashion, thrown completely away, be worn for show (e.g. a show of wealth) or be worn purely for personal pleasure. The ordinary ring is non-singular and functions like a sign; it is an object of consumption (1981: 66). Baudrillard goes on to suggest that much of the thinking about "needs" fails to take into account the systematicity of subject–object relations and the ways in which the different logics of consumption and exchange are confused and conflated. What is the solution, then, if consumption is to be elucidated? With a rather grand gesture, Baudrillard says "It thus proves necessary to reconstruct social logic entirely" (1981: 72). This is to be done not merely by arguing that there is no such thing as the object (because we deal with the object as sign) but that there is also no such thing as the individual. Baudrillard's structuralist Marxism here is moving a very long way from Marx, even given all the comments concerning production. Following Lévi-Strauss and others, Baudrillard is suggesting here that the individual subject is preceded by the social system: "Even before survival has been assured, every group of individuals experiences a vital pressure to produce themselves meaningfully in a system of exchange and relationships" (1981: 74). Instead of the liberal-humanist position, whereby human beings contain and express their inner and innate identities, Baudrillard is arguing that people are only ever given their identities by the social systems that precede them. A "language" of exchange precedes the subject, because the subject can be one of the signifiers involved in the system, the subject is identified by the system (e.g. in terms of marriage or kinship systems) and the subject can be one of the "significant elements" within the hierarchy of the system. The argument runs that goods and products also enter the system like the human subject, thus consumption equals exchange (1981: 75). Just as language is not constructed instant by instant by the individual speech act, so consumption is not constructed or ordered instant by instant by individual need. The subject is born into language and consumption exists and occurs within a field of differences and codes:

> The circulation, purchase, sale, appropriation of differentiated goods and signs/objects today constitute our language, our code, the code by which the entire society *communicates* and converses. Such is the structure of consumption, its language [*langue*], by comparison with which individual needs and pleasures [*jouissances*] are merely speech effects.
>
> (1998b: 79–80)

Baudrillard's analyses of consumption as functioning as a differential sign-system is elaborated and further theorized in *For a Critique of the Political Economy of the Sign*. This collection of essays from the late 1960s and early 1970s analyses the sign form in a way analogous to earlier Marxist analyses of the commodity form. At times supplementing *The System of Objects* and *Consumer Society*, at other times presenting similar arguments from a less theoretically coherent perspective, these essays provide a detailed alliance of Marxist and semiotic thought. While it is beyond the scope of this chapter to provide an in-depth survey of these essays, it can be noted that the political framework of these analyses also functions as a boundary marker of the ultimate stretching of Marxist thought beyond which Baudrillard may occasionally go in this period, but always with his return to Marx and theories of production in mind.

THE CRITIQUE OF MARX

From being a touchstone to the theories of consumption in the early cluster of works, *production* after 1972 becomes instead the *aporia* or "blind spot" of Marxist thought. Production is perceived to be a concept which dominates Marxist thought. Because of this domination it becomes a limit to the system of Marxist analyses – in other words, Marxism cannot see beyond production. This is why it is a "blind spot".

The Mirror of Production, while developing many of the ideas in the early cluster of work, is far more of a radical break with those works than is often realized. In *The Mirror of Production*, Baudrillard attacks the onto-logical (how we exist in the world) and epistemological (how we know the world) Marxist notions of production that lead to production, circumscribing "... the entire history of man in a gigantic simulation model" (1975: 33). In many ways this attack is far more blunt-edged than closely detailed, partly because Baudrillard is trying to tackle an entire system broadside on, and partly because he is using deconstruc-tive logic which isn't always very clear. But it is this deconstruction of Marxism that gives the argument its radicalism, and we shall try to clarify this strand of the overall argument.

Baudrillard returns to the building blocks of Marxist theory in *The Mirror of Production*. In particular, he is interested in the dialectic of quality and quantity (1975: 25). Comparing the notion of quality as it relates to pre-industrialized modes of production (where "quality" equals the fact that the worker is involved with the product from beginning to end) and quantity as relating to mass production (since the energy to work is sold to someone else and the worker just repeti-tively performs the same task with no pleasure or pride in the final product), Baudrillard then thinks about these in relation to use-value and exchange-value. Thus, "In the subsequent capitalist mode of production labour is analyzed under a double form" (1975: 26). For Marx, labour can be either "concrete and special" (with the production of use-value) or "abstract, universal and homogeneous" (with the production of exchange value) (1975: 26). Marx argues that use-value produces exchange value:

> The product ... is a use-value, as yarn, for example, or boots. But although boots are, to some extent, the basis of social progress, and our capitalist is decidedly in favour of progress, he does not manufacture boots for their own sake ... Use-values are produced by capitalists only because and, in so far as they form the material substratum of exchange-value, are the bearers of exchange-value.
>
> (1975: 293)

The narrative of the shift in modes of production emphasizes the changes in labour relations in the eighteenth century. But Baudrillard argues that it is not the shift away from pre-industrialized modes of production that leads to the universalization of the notion of labour itself. Instead, the universalized notion of labour is generated by the "structural articulation" of the two terms "quality" and "quantity":

> Work is really universalized at the base of this "fork," not only as market value but as human value. Ideology always thus proceeds by a binary, structural scission [splitting], which works here to universalize the dimension of labour. By dividing ... quantitative labour spreads throughout the field of possibility.
>
> (1975: 27)

This is an incredibly difficult point to grasp, because Baudrillard is suggesting, as with Lévi-Strauss's notion of the incest taboo (see Chapter 6), that there is an "originary" articulation of an impossible binary opposition here. Another way of putting this is that a whole system of thought – here it is Marxism – is put into motion by a contradiction. Thus, quality does not precede quantity, as Marx argues, where quality is real, concrete, derived from nature, and quantity is abstract and artificially generated. Or, where quality is the product followed by the craftsperson from beginning to end (the entire boot), and quantity is the abstracted sold labour (the eyelet in a boot punched at a machine over and over again). Rather, the structural system generated by the articulation of these oppositions enables us to articulate the notion of the universal necessity for productive labour in the first place. But such a structural system, and any "universal" notion, will be in themselves "abstract". We then (as Marxists) read back into pre-Capitalist modes of production the notions of concrete, real, qualitative labour, and lose sight of the fact that all of these notions derive from our later abstract system. Baudrillard's deconstructive argument has radical implications for many (if not all) of the founding concepts of Marxism. He summarizes his analysis of this structural articulation as follows:

> ... "concrete" is an abuse of the word. It seems opposed to the abstract at the base of the fork [between quality and quantity], but in fact the fork is what establishes the abstraction. The autonomization of labour is sealed in the play of the two from the abstract to the concrete, from the qualitative to the quantitative, from the exchange value to the use value of labour. In this structuralized play of signifiers, the fetishism of labour and productivity crystallizes.
>
> (1975: 27)

For Baudrillard, Marxism is bound up with a narrative where humanity is regarded as a productive community of beings who are condemned or saved by labour depending on the ideological system in operation. In other words, the human subject realizes himself or herself in labour. We have already briefly examined the master/slave narrative in Hegel, where the seeds of the slave's salvation are sown precisely through work. But what we haven't examined in any great depth are models of human society that do not construct themselves via productive labour. Such models, Baudrillard argues – for example, "primitive" or "archaic" societies – would contradict the founding premise of productive labour.

Baudrillard is keen to maintain the opposition between material and symbolic wealth. The former is produced within a teleological system – always gaining more, always becoming more productive, always realizing more capital, and so on. Symbolic wealth, however, is non-teleological and non-productive, coming as it does from interchanges of destruction, abandonment, giving and transgression. *Symbolic* wealth, as its name suggests, simply does not signify in the same way as material wealth. To take one example – with the emblazoned copper objects of the Canadian northwest coast Haida and Kwakiutl that Marcel Mauss discusses briefly in *The Gift*, we find symbolic wealth may have an existence, *a being as such*, alien to that of material wealth; the copper objects may speak or grumble, demand to be kept warm, given away or destroyed; they may attract other copper objects, but not in a simplistic causal relationship, because of the intricate interconnections of object, spirit and title (Mauss 1990: 45). The crucial factor in symbolic wealth is one of relationship: it is the process of each particular "exchange" that creates symbolic meaning, including the reciprocal recognition from other people, spirits and objects (which are an amalgam of these categories in the first place). In many respects Baudrillard is maintaining a "purist" reading of Marx here to push the logic of Marxism to its limits without turning it into something radically different, e.g. the excessiveness of Bataille's theories that promote transgression, destruction, waste, and so on. One of the limit strategies used is that of examining the ways in which Marxist concepts are "universalized" in the process of critiquing bourgeois thought. In other words, such concepts are not regarded as historically situated interpretive devices, but universal categories. We can see the problem by briefly thinking about Hegel's *Phenomenology of Spirit* here;

the dialectical movement of the *Phenomenology* is always towards "Absolute Spirit"; but, right from the start, "Absolute Spirit" is encoded in the naïve position of the subject, since no position can be entirely "outside" the dialectic, and the end point fuels or drives the beginning. With the universalization of Marxist concepts, Baudrillard argues that there is a threefold result: the concepts cease to be analytical and become "religious" or mystical; the concepts take on a scientific cast; the concepts become representative of reality/truth, not interpretive (1975: 48). As universalized concepts, like "Absolute Spirit", they become the goal and the driving force in an enclosed system of thought. Other societies, e.g. so-called "primitive" or "archaic" societies, must, within this enclosed system, be presented as somehow "embryonic". Baudrillard argues that we can see the limits of Marxist thought precisely at this failed point of contact (failed because the Other is interpreted via the same): "There is *neither a mode of production nor production* in primitive societies. There is *no dialectic* and *no unconscious* in primitive societies. These concepts analyze our own societies, which are ruled by political economy" (1975: 49). In the previous chapter we discussed how Baudrillard is able to make such interpretive claims about other societies himself; here the point is that, in bringing Marxist thought up against an alien Other, Marxism is shown to be a local phenomenon, if one of great explanatory power, not a set of universals.

SUMMARY

Baudrillard's attempt to articulate a structural Marxism has been shown to turn into the critique of Marx from 1972 onwards. This chapter has examined the way that Baudrillard's description of the everyday experience of the jungle of objects prefigures the critique of Marx from the position of a new theory of consumption. In other words, we have seen how Baudrillard maps out the contemporary world of consumerist objects using the logic of Marxism (especially use-value and exchange-value), but then goes on to realize that there are gaps in the Marxist account, such as the astronomical rise in wages and the negativity and oppression of the consumer product turning into a positive factor in people's lives. We have also seen how for Baudrillard the process whereby the object is divorced from production and symbolic value means that the object now functions like a sign. The critique of Marx which follows depends upon this insight, as well as analyses of notions of quality/quantity and the opposition between material and symbolic wealth.

5

SIMULATION AND THE HYPERREAL

This chapter explores two of the central ideas in Baudrillard's later work: simulation and the hyperreal. The chapter puts these ideas into their historical context, as well as relating them to postmodernism, war and film. Finally, the chapter examines some of the theoretical interconnections between Baudrillard and French theorists Michel Foucault and Guy Debord.

WATERGATE

On 17 June 1972, five men broke into the offices of a building called the "Watergate" in Washington, DC. Over the next two years, the US President, Richard Nixon, would attempt to cover up the involvement of himself and his men in this deed. What unfolded during those two years, instead, was the recognition that corruption in the White House ran deeper than anyone had imagined possible: the attempt to bug the Democrats' offices in Watergate was one in a series of criminal offences that included a plan to firebomb a liberal think tank called The Brookings Institution, the illegal bugging and burglary of people connected with the release of the Pentagon Papers in 1971, and a whole host of presidential campaign "dirty tricks" (see the 1976 film *All the President's Men*). The investigations that followed led President Nixon to resign – the first President to do so – rather than face

impeachment, in August 1974. A whole host of Nixon's closest advisers – the most senior men in government – were eventually charged with criminal offences and imprisoned. With Gerald Ford's speech, as he took over as the thirty-eighth President of the United States, it could be argued that this damaging scandal was over; other "gates" have followed – Iran-, Iraq- and Whitewater-gate – but, as Fred Emery notes, Watergate "is still the mother of all 'gates'" (Emery, 1995: xiv). The Watergate narrative can be summarized succinctly: a burglary ruptures the pretence that the government in charge of a Capitalist democracy is actually law-abiding; the scandal of a government going "off the rails" and the attempted cover-up is gradually made public, until the nation's legal processes take over, removing or destroying the corrupt men in office, so that democracy is once again restored.

But this is not Baudrillard's point of view. In his *Simulations*, he argues:

> *Watergate is not a scandal*: this is what must be said at all cost, for this is what everyone is concerned to conceal, this dissimulation masking a strengthening of morality, a moral panic as we approach the primal (mise en) scène of capital: its instantaneous cruelty, its incomprehensible ferocity, its fundamental immorality – this is what is scandalous ...

> (1983b: 29)

Baudrillard seems to be reversing the Watergate situation here. He suggests that it is not the corruption of government that is scandalous, but the fact that what Watergate reveals about government is a "truth" that is then covered up by the suggestion that this event is an *aberration* not a constitutive "fact". In other words, instead of Watergate revealing a morally superior system going wrong (Capitalism controlled by democracy breaks down), Baudrillard argues that Watergate reveals that "Capital doesn't give a damn about the idea of the contract which is imputed to it – it is a monstrous unprincipled undertaking, nothing more" (1983b: 29). So the scandal arises, for Baudrillard, not because of the Watergate break-in, not because of the cover-up that follows, but when the revelation that government is unprincipled is itself covered up by the so-called return to order with the end of the Nixon regime and the inauguration of President Ford.

If we simply had the above reversal of values to deal with (one scandal replaced by another), then Baudrillard's account of Watergate would be easy to understand. But there is more to his account than an inversion of morality and moral lessons. Baudrillard's first mention of Watergate is far more complex: "Watergate. Same scenario as Disneyland (an imaginary effect concealing that reality no more exists outside than inside the bounds of the artificial perimeter) ..." (1983b: 26). How can the most disturbing political scandal of the 1970s be compared with Disneyland? And what does this comparison tell us about postmodernism?

POSTMODERNISM

Roland Barthes once described the literary text as "a tissue of quotations". This description could have been used just as accurately for the postmodern. A postmodern text, building, performance, and so on, is usually a mixture of styles, drawing upon different historical movements and features to produce a hybrid form. This is in direct opposition to modernism, which rejected the past to build a new, enclosed style of its own. Postmodern form is open-ended, self-reflective (in that the form may "quote" itself) and dynamic in the sense of welcoming incorporation of its own features into other postmodern texts, buildings, etc. Critics still argue about when the postmodern began. Generally, the term gathered pace during the 1950s and 1960s, coming to the fore in the 1970s with the appearance of influential French theorist Jean-François Lyotard's *La Condition postmoderne* (1979; English edition 1984). However, if one major historical event marks the shift into the postmodern world, it may be the Vietnam War (1959–1973), which led to a widespread distrust of authority and technology, at the same time promoting the televisual experience of reality. In literature, key postmodern novelists include Thomas Pynchon (e.g. *The Crying of Lot 49*, 1966) and Don DeLillo (e.g. *White Noise*, 1984; Picador edition 1986).

To answer these questions we need to think closely, first about the Disneyland example and then about the way in which the other "examples" in *Simulations* sketch out a highly critical vision of a postmodern world.

DISNEYLAND

If we think about a place such as Disneyland, in the US, we tend to think in terms of a fantasy representation of reality, a simulation of the real taken to extremes (such as the "fairy-tale" Disney castle based upon buildings found throughout Europe). But Baudrillard regards Disneyland, and the country that surrounds it, as partaking of the "third order" of simulation. A first-order simulation would be where the representation of the real (say, a novel, a painting or a map) is obviously just that: an artificial representation. A second-order simulation, however, *blurs the boundaries between reality and representation*. Baudrillard points us towards Borges' fable "Of Exactitude in Science", where "...the cartographers of the Empire draw up a map so detailed that it ends up exactly covering the territory ..." (1983b: 1); in other words, the "map" and reality can no longer be discerned, so the map has become, in a sense, as real as the real. But third-order simulation goes beyond these positions; *third-order simulation produces a "hyperreal"*, or "...the generation by models of a real without origin or reality ..." (1983b: 2). In a reversal of order, in third-order simulation, the model precedes the real (e.g. the map precedes the territory) – but this doesn't mean that there is a blurring between reality and representation; rather, there is a detachment from both of these, whereby *the reversal becomes irrelevant*. Baudrillard suggests that hyperreality is produced algorithmically (or via mathematical formulae), like the virtual reality of computer code; that is to say, detached from notions of mimesis and representation and implicated, for example, in the world of mathematical formulae. The important and disturbing point to all this is that the hyperreal doesn't exist in the realm of good and evil, because it is measured as such in terms of its performativity – how well does it work or operate?

THIRD-ORDER SIMULATION

With first- and second-order simulation, the real still exists, and we measure the success of simulation against the real. Baudrillard's worry with third-order simulation is that the model now generates what he calls "hyperreality" – that is, a world without a real origin. So, with third order

To comprehend the complexities in Baudrillard's concept of the hyperreal, it is necessary to think through the concrete examples scattered throughout the two essays that make up the English publication of *Simulations*. It is worth thinking through the references to medicine, the military and religion, and the notions of simulation that are explored. In a section called "The Divine Irreference of Images", Baudrillard discusses the difference between feigning/dissimulating and simulation; with the former, there is a relationship with absence and presence, or a relationship with the "true" state of affairs. Dissimulation is a form of pretence, or a covering of one's real feelings. Baudrillard says: "To dissimulate is to feign not to have what one has" (1983b: 5). Thus, someone who is hungry, for example, may pretend not to be, perhaps to maintain a certain image of control. Baudrillard argues that, in dissimulation, the reality principle is left intact – for example, someone goes to bed and feigns an illness simply by saying that he or she feels unwell. But with the *simulation* of an illness, the person in bed actually produces some of the symptoms – for example, excessive sneezing. In the latter case, how are we to know what the real state of affairs actually is? Does the person have flu or not, if we can witness them sneezing away? In the example of someone feigning an illness, with no obvious symptoms, we can probably verify that they have some other reason to lie about their true state (like a child who doesn't want to go to school). The point is that we can identify that the subject actually has good health and that they are feigning its absence. In other words, we can still negotiate the differences between a true and false state of affairs. With simulation, we can no longer negotiate the differences, so the differences themselves are threatened. If this logic is taken any further, then medical science is itself brought into question: "...if any symptom can be 'produced', and can no longer be accepted as a fact of nature, then every illness may be considered simulatable and simulated, and medicine loses its meaning since it only knows how to treat 'true' illnesses by their objective causes" (1983b: 5–6). Baudrillard gives two further examples of this blurring of the boundaries between true and false, with examples of simulation in the army and the church. In the past, Baudrillard argues, the army would "unmask" those subjects guilty of simulating an illness or madness, for example, to get out of a particular duty (or to get out of the army altogether); the subjects would then be punished for their misdeeds. However, in the present, Baudrillard argues that the army now attempts to "reform" simulators – in other words, treat their "illnesses" as real and return them eventually to duty. In this reformation, the reality principle has broken down, because there is no attempt to look beyond the simulated symptoms for a "true" state of affairs: the symptoms are always already the performative truth of the subject, regardless of whether he or she is ill or not.

PERFORMATIVE KNOWLEDGE

In Lyotard's *The Postmodern Condition*, technology is discussed as something that optimizes performance; that is to say, the attainment of the maximum output for the minimum input. There is no notion here of technology leading to something more profound – such as a deeper understanding of the universe, through the use of computers for example – just a more efficient or productive way of technology functioning. Philosophical ideals such as "truth" or "ethics" are subordinated in the postmodern to performativity: if it works, it is good. Lyotard argued in the 1970s that higher education would come to be dominated by performativity: skills needed to increase the "performativity of the social system" would be prioritized. For example, the teaching of computer sciences and genetic engineering would take priority over traditional subjects such as philosophy and the arts.

Baudrillard's final example is that of the religious image, and the danger of a monotheistic (single) God being scattered via a multitude of icons or simulacra. In such a process, the "true" God would be replaced by a series of simulated gods. Baudrillard argues that it cannot be quite so simple, because the icons would then be dissimulating (that is, feigning) that they haven't the power of the one God, therefore being in relation to the absent God (proving that God exists and that God potentially has ultimate power). Instead, the problem with the icons is that they have a facility "...of effacing God from the conscious-ness of men" (1983b: 8) in the process suggesting that "... ultimately there has never been any God, that only the simulacrum exists, indeed that God himself has only ever been his own simulacrum" (1983b: 8).

Baudrillard calls Disneyland a third-order simulation, which can now be linked to Watergate. It is easy to think about Disneyland as a second-order simulation, where fake castles look more real than the real, because they embody all of our childish and romantic notions of what a castle should ideally look like, and the machinery of representa-tion is so well hidden that reality and representation blur together. But the implications of Disneyland as third-order simulation are much harder to come to grips with. Baudrillard argues that

> Disneyland is there to conceal the fact that it is the "real" country, all of "real" America, which *is* Disneyland ... Disneyland is presented as imaginary in order to make us believe that the rest is real, when in fact all of Los Angeles and the America surrounding it are no longer real, but of the order of the hyperreal and of simulation.
>
> (1983b: 25)

Baudrillard makes the comparison with prisons, arguing that prisons hide the fact that we are incarcerated in society; in other words, we believe in our freedom precisely because we lock criminals away and lose sight of the structural similarities between the two social realms. This was a point that Foucault made explicitly in his *Surveiller et punir* in 1975 (translated by Alan Sheridan as *Discipline and Punish: The Birth of the Prison*). Foucault made famous the notion of micro-powers in society functioning like the panopticon; that is to say, the famous prison plan devised by the English philosopher Jeremy Bentham (1748–1832), which gives the notion of a discipline mechanism through the potential of permanent surveillance. Foucault's description of the panopticon is worth quoting at some length here (although we will also examine Baudrillard's critique of it at the end of this chapter):

> ...at the periphery, an annular building; at the centre, a tower; this tower is pierced with wide windows that open onto the inner side of the ring; the periph-eric building is divided into cells, each of which extends the whole width of the

building; they have two windows, one on the inside, corresponding to the windows of the tower; the other, on the outside, allows the light to cross the cell from one end to the other ... By the effect of backlighting, one can observe from the tower, standing out precisely against the light, the small captive shadows in the cells of the periphery. They are like so many cages, so many small theatres, in which each actor is alone, perfectly individualized and constantly visible.

(Foucault, 1979: 200)

Foucault picked up on Bentham's notion of panopticism, whereby society no longer functions according to the traditional model of sovereign power, or power inflicted directly and physically on the people from above, but instead intersects with every subject through the *relations* of discipline (Foucault, 1979: 208). In relation to the comments made in "Why Baudrillard?" (see p. 3) and Chapter 1, this is a structuralist notion of how power operates in society – think back to the notion of the indicative Monnet Plans, which are brought into being by each individual in society not by some order from above. Baudrillard's point in *Simulations* is that society can only function if the subject believes that rationality holds sway, and discipline, childishness, madness and so on are seen to be elsewhere. Or, to put this another way, society needs to believe that the sovereign power of rationality holds sway. Thus he calls Disneyland "...a deterrence machine set up in order to rejuvenate in reverse the fiction of the real" (1983b: 25). What he means by this is that Disneyland exists to convince us that rationality is outside the walls of its childish domain, rather than the fact that rationality has been replaced by childishness everywhere. This is why Watergate gets compared to Disneyland. Watergate generates a scandal that exists to rejuvenate or regenerate "a moral and political principle ..." (1983b: 27). The principle is that government is fundamentally moral in its approaches, and that society shares that morality; but such a notion is undermined by the obfuscation or obscuring actions by government forces in America at the time (such as the FBI) and the way in which the journalists had to take as devious an approach to the event as the people who were implicated. Baudrillard thus accuses the famous *Washington Post* journalists Bob Woodward and Carl Bernstein, of employing methods analogous to those of the CIA (1983b: 27). But this is quite an astounding claim, which would seem to conflate two journalists trying to get at the truth with those corrupt and immoral officials of the Nixon administration who were clearly intent on breaking the law (and, in the process, regarding themselves as somehow above the law). This is a claim that Baudrillard can only justify and explain with reference to Capitalism and notions of left- and right-wing political actions. Quoting French philosopher Pierre Bourdieu, and his view that relations of force are not only bound up with dissimulation, but actually gain power through dissimulation (e.g. a multinational corporation claiming an ethical policy towards the environment in the West while doing the complete opposite in the Developing World), Baudrillard follows this through with the argument that capital, which is "immoral" (placing itself beyond questions of good and evil), can only function through dissimulation. Capital therefore needs a moral "front" with which to present itself to the world. Any regeneration of this moral "front" thus increases the power of capital to misrepresent itself. Thus the claim that Woodward and Bernstein further "...the order of capital" (1983b: 27). For Baudrillard, Woodward and Bernstein (and, indeed, Bourdieu), all make the same mistake: they believe in the "rationality" of capital (even if this is simply where they want capital to "end up", so to speak) when Baudrillard regards capital as being divorced from rationality. This leaves us in the position whereby we can't tell if right-wing actions – such as "Deep Throat" in the Watergate case, who leaked key facts to the *Washington Post* journalists – are for left- or right-wing results, and vice versa (especially if we accept the argument that the moral regeneration of government increases the power of capital as such). This would seem to leave us in a frightening abyss, where the hyperreal produces a society of surfaces, performativity and a fragmentation or fracturing of rationality. Such a world has been called by many critics "the postmodern".

POSTMODERN 1970S

One of the ironies of the Watergate period, with its endemic corruption, is that the Nixon administration was bringing the Vietnam War to an end. In fact, Henry Kissinger's premature announcement in October 1972 that peace in Vietnam was at hand, while far from the truth, signalled correctly the direction in which the US government was heading. Just five months after the Watergate burglary, the Nixon administration was re-elected with a huge majority; in Vietnam, the peace deal that Kissinger had hinted at finally became a reality after the problematic but politically effective "Christmas bombing", leading to a Nobel prize for Kissinger and the Communist leader Le Duc Tho (Emery, 1995: 231). Eventually, Congress would demand the withdrawal from South Vietnam of all American troops, and the war would be over, except in one of the places it still seems to rage to this day: the American psyche. Vietnam has been called the first "television war", referring to the way in which images of its death and destruction permeated the West via this dominating technology. In many respects, reporters would never have such freedom to roam the battlefield again, as military powers realized the potential of controlling or directing the media reporting of war. Subsequent wars, especially the Gulf War, have all been discussed as being part of a massive desire for catharsis, a healing moment when US power reasserts itself after the failures in Vietnam. But this, in turn, fails to come to terms with the Vietnam War "itself" and a series of questions left unanswered: What was the war all about? Why did so many Americans die in a situation that didn't seem to make sense to so many people back home? Was the war responsible for the rise of student and other activists in the West, for example, with May 1968? And what was America's position as a "superpower" after the defeat in Vietnam? Many more questions remain unanswered, but in the media, especially film, such questions became issues that were constantly explored, that constantly circulated. In Chapter 1 we noted the way in which Baudrillard regarded the media in May 1968 as short-circuiting notions of symbolic exchange, a kind of divorce from actions and language that can change the world; in a sense, we can say that by May 1968 the media had already entered the world of third-order simulation, where it didn't matter if it represented revolution as a good or bad thing, or even if it portrayed the events as truly revolutionary or simply a temporary student uprising (even given the associated strikes, etc.). This gives us a hint as to how to theorize Baudrillard's notion of the media in Vietnam as already being something other than a true or false representation of the situation on the ground. What happens during and after Vietnam is in some sense for Baudrillard already hyperreal, as with Watergate, and this hyperreality is a way of describing the postmodern situation in the 1970s.

WAR AND FILM

The first essay in Baudrillard's *Simulations*, "The Precession of Simulacra", actually derives from a book published in France in 1981 called *Simulacres et Simulation*. In the latter there is a chapter on Francis Ford Coppola's Vietnam War film *Apocalypse Now* (1979), which gives further insight into third-order simulation. Baudrillard argues that war and film are both, in the American world, hyperreal: both are theorized as *tests*. What exactly does Baudrillard mean by this? He suggests that the Vietnam War was like a film before it was even filmed, because it was composed of "special effects" and technological and psychedelic fantasy (1994a: 59). Further, the war became a test-site or testing ground, whereby the Americans could test new weapons technologies and technologies of power (which, unlike the Gulf War, were ironically not of much use because of the problematic terrain in Vietnam). Baudrillard argues:

> Coppola does nothing but that: test cinema's power of intervention, test the impact of a cinema that has become an immeasurable machinery of special effects. In this sense, his film is really the extension of war through other means, the pinnacle of this failed war, and its apotheosis. The war became film, the film becomes war, the two are joined by their common hemorrhage into technology.
>
> (1994a: 59)

Coppola doesn't just recreate the war in realistic ways, e.g. the napalmed Philippine forests and villages (this, in itself, would be second-order simulation); instead, he reveals the similitude between his psychedelic series of excesses that made the film (e.g. massive economic and nervous expenditure, excessive destruction of the environment for very little return, and so on) and those that took place during – or "as" – the Vietnam War. In other words, while the war had a *physical* manifestation, that of massive and excessive expenditure, it took place as a *psychical* process: the film *Apocalypse Now* is just as much a part of that physical and psychical process as the war itself: they are "cut from the same cloth", as Baudrillard says (1994a: 60). For Baudrillard, what is hyperreal about this situation is the reversibility between destruction and production: the war ends and American economic aid is "immediately" forthcoming; the film destroys to produce itself. In both instances, destruction and production are interchangeable.

LYOTARD

In his accounts of the Vietnam War and *Apocalypse Now*, Baudrillard is articulating a postmodern process whereby the "grand narratives" of progress, technology and rationalism are replaced by the hyperreal world of third-order simulation: an excessive world of expenditure and psychedelic spectacle. This is in accord with a survey of the state of knowledge in Western society at the close of the 1970s written by Jean-François Lyotard – a survey called *The Postmodern Condition*. Lyotard's notion of the loss of the power of the "grand narratives" that derive from the Enlightenment is fundamentally a positive one, compared with Baudrillard's cynicism and critical edge, especially concerning Baudrillard's notion that the overall effect of the hyperreal is to prove the system by the crisis (1983b: 36). Lyotard regards the postmodern 1970s as moving towards new technologies which all focus on issues of language: computer languages, communication theories, the return in philosophy to language with the work of thinkers such as Wittgenstein (especially his ideas concerning "language games", or a way of thinking through linguistic models and how they function in everyday life), and associated technologies, to take just a few examples. However, rather than regarding such language-based models as generating a hyperreal, Lyotard breaks down models of information into those fields that reject narrative (such as science) and those that are narrative-based. He does this to argue a complex case, whereby science is shown to be ultimately basing itself upon a higher level of narrative – a "metanarrative" – that legitimizes notions of progress in society through scientific means. Lyotard argues that in the 1970s there is a waning of the power of such metanarratives, and it can be argued that the Vietnam War is an example of this, as people gradually began to be sceptical of the political metanarratives (that the fall of Vietnam to Communist control would mean the uncontainable spread of communism throughout Southeast Asia) and the scientific/technological metanarratives (that America's superior technologies could end the war). What is beginning to happen with this waning of metanarrative power, according to Lyotard, is the splintering of knowledge into a kind of utopian space where people can creatively leap from one knowledge domain to another to come up with radically new ideas or theories (see Connor, 1989: 33). Baudrillard's vision is much more bleak: he would reject the notion that such a "utopian space" can develop as long as information in general is constructed and conveyed via the hyperreal. That is to say, he questions the very grounds of creative new theories when knowledge is produced by models, and those models are controlled by governments and media groups. Baudrillard's analysis of how such hyperreality functions can be found over a decade later with the Gulf War texts eventually published in English as *The Gulf War Did Not Take Place*.

THE GULF WAR

In his introduction to *The Gulf War Did Not Take Place*, Paul Patton narrates an absurd moment in the reporting of the war when the news channel CNN switched to a group of reporters "live" in the Gulf to ask them what was happening, only to discover that they were watching CNN to find out themselves (Baudrillard, 1995: 2). This absurd moment reveals the detachment from the real, and the production of "reality" with third-order simulation: news is generated by news, or the source of the news is also the news. This isn't to suggest a degradation of news information – the notion that the first piece of coverage is closest to what is really happening, the next bit slightly less accurate because based upon the first, and so on. If anything, there is nothing to "degrade" because news isn't being generated by some singular event. Rather, news is producing the "reality" of the war, not only for viewers, but also for those involved. Propaganda is thereby taken to a new level: it isn't a case of misrepresenting what is actually happening somewhere in a different way; more a case of constructing what *will be* happening in advance (that is, what will be happening to the troops on the other side of the conflict), so that it *does* happen. Hyperreal propaganda is therefore like the Cold War, another war that did not take place in the sense of physical combat among comparative powers. It is fought through projections and simulations of what might be (e.g. Armageddon), precisely to make sure that a particular outcome does happen: the collapse of the Soviet threat.

Baudrillard's three essays in *The Gulf War Did Not Take Place* all have one aim: to show that the Gulf War was hyperreal, and that war in the conventional sense never actually occurred. One of the key quotes from the book, which Patton also uses in his introduction, suggests that the Gulf War functioned like the flow of capital:

> Just as wealth is no longer measured by the ostentation of wealth but by the secret circulation of speculative capital, so war is not measured by being waged but by its speculative unfolding in an abstract, electronic and informational space, the same space in which capital moves.
>
> (1995: 56)

In *Simulations*, Baudrillard argued that the hyperreal was generated in effect by computer software or analogous systems; with the Gulf War, Baudrillard argues that the war was preprogrammed by the Americans, and that its "events" unfolded according to that programme. Thus the absurdities, for example, of the fear of an enemy that was technologically inferior and in the final instance didn't even exist (the withdrawal of the elite Iraqi troops before the endgame). But these were not absurdities according to the hyperreal programme of what should be happening and what sort of responses should be generated. If we analyse the virtual war (i.e. the television war) as being of the second order of simulation – that is to say, it represents a blurring between reality and representation (an example of this would be missiles that were practically useless, being represented as a genuine threat) – then we would expect at some stage a progression to a "real" war with potentially apocalyptical consequences. One of the proofs of the Gulf War's hyperreality is the fact that this "progression" doesn't take place, it remains in the informational space: "We are no longer in a logic of the passage from virtual to actual but in a hyperrealist logic of the deterrence of the real by the virtual" (1995: 27). This virtual war is symptomatic, for Baudrillard, of an illness that it is quite difficult to interpret, except to say that an entire culture (the West) is now geared towards deception, in other words the production of virtual reality and the "counterfeit" (1995: 43). The Gulf War doesn't have an objective in the traditional military sense of the word. Instead, the war is about itself – it is a self-reflexive act or test, to see if war is possible in the postmodern world: "... what is at stake ... is war itself: its status, its meaning, its future. It is beholden not to have an objective but to prove its very existence ..." (1995: 32). One of the key deceptions of the Gulf War was that it was a "clean" war, devoid almost entirely of bloodshed and suffering. Baudrillard's response to this is the cutting phrase that "A clean war ends up in an oil slick" (1995: 43). Yet this suggests that critics such as Baudrillard can differentiate between the hyperreal and the real; that we are not as caught up in the post-modern state of third-order simulation as Baudrillard initially suggests. At the same time as he seems to desire that an "event" will override "virtuality", Baudrillard is arguing that there is no such thing as the real or the true. What is going on here? I would argue that one of the problems in reading Baudrillard is the intersection of perform-ance and critique in his work: *The Gulf War Did Not Take Place* is both a postmodern performance, taking the logic of hyperreality to its extreme (thus the Gulf War did not take place because it was nothing but simulation), and it is a critique of hyperreality (just as in Chapter 1 Baudrillard critiques the media representation of May 1968). At times, performance and critique are at odds with one another in Baudrillard's work; at other times, he is writing at the limit of ideas, pushing them until they almost shatter under the strain. It is this limit-writing that makes Baudrillard a radical thinker, but also one firmly in the French intellectual tradition of thinkers who push ideas to the limit (see Chapter 7). This contradictory space of thinking (and writing as performance that leads to a fragmentation of ideas) may in itself be seen as part of postmodern existence.

ENDGAME – LIMITS

In a section of *Simulations* called "The End of the Panopticon", Baudrillard takes care to distance himself from the theory with which his work intersects at key moments, and this distancing is designed so as to get as close to the thought of hyperreality as possible. Two of the thinkers "rejected" or critiqued are Foucault and Debord; in particular, Baudrillard wants to get beyond a moralistic notion of the "spectacular" implicit in both (see "Society of the Spectacle", p. 99). In a dense burst of statements and ideas, this going beyond is realized through an early fly-on-the-wall television documentary produced in the US in 1971. The documentary followed the Loud family for seven months of continuous filming, including the break-up of the family, inevitably raising issues of surveillance, media pressure and the notion of the observer affecting the observed. Baudrillard's analysis of this situation could be profitably retheorized in relation to the fetishization of such a situation as it currently exists in different forms on the Internet with live digital camera feeds.

Baudrillard argues that the Loud documentary was not simply about voyeurism; that is, a relationship between spectacle and spectator that is one-way, with the spectator "spying" on the subjects via television cameras. Instead, by arguing that the documentary took place as if the cameras were not there, the director signalled a utopian ideal whereby the distance between spectacle and spectator was reduced to zero, or collapsed. In other words, with voyeurism, however intimate the scene being watched, there is always a perspectival distance, perhaps a window separating the subjects, or the distance between scene and camera, and so on. But if the cameras were "not there", so to speak, then the collapsed distance means that the viewers were also in the scene: "It is this utopia, this paradox that fascinated 20 million viewers, much more than the 'perverse' pleasure of prying" (1983b: 50). The viewers are absent and present, at a distance and up close; they enjoy the thrill of this hyperreal situation: hyperreal because they cannot say that one position is real and another false (both subject positions have been collapsed and distanced at the same time). A helpful analogy is that of the close-up photograph: when we get "too close" to an object, we sometimes have trouble even distinguishing what the object is. In that sense, we cannot say that we have a grasp on the "real" object in front of us. The hyperreal, in relation to this analogy, is like the extreme close-up and an extreme long-distance photograph at the same time. That is to say, there is no longer a third, normative position of realistic perspective. The notion of total involvement or immersion combined with alienating detachment is also perceived, according to Baudrillard, in such television subgenres as pornography.

In the collapsing of perspectival space, Baudrillard distances himself in this text from the theoretical implications of Foucault's use of the panopticon, where society is structured by surveillance apparatus, however "internalized". In perspectival space, there is still the play of the opposition seeing/being seen; with hyperreality, any family can stand in for the Louds on television, and the Louds on television are any family; the active *seeing* and the passive *being seen* are one and the same position. Another way of thinking about this is in terms of the decentred structure, as it becomes impossible to locate the traditional nodes of power and subjection with the collapse of perspectival space; instead, there is a circulation of positions which, again, all appear interchangeable. For example, as the distinctive modern city shopping district gives way to suburban hypermarkets, the geographical space of the latter is interchangeable and almost "out of place" because it could be anywhere. Baudrillard argues:

> Television, in the case of the Louds for example, is no longer a spectacular medium. We are no longer in the society of spectacle which the situationists talked about, nor in the specific types of alienation and repression which this implied.

> (1983b: 54)

This reference to the "society of spectacle" and the distancing from it is exceptionally important, as Baudrillard has highlighted another key 1970s intertext for an understanding of his work, regardless of the critique made in *Simulations*.

SOCIETY OF THE SPECTACLE

Guy Debord first published his book *The Society of the Spectacle* in 1967, whereupon it became one of the key texts for many students and thinkers involved in the May 1968 uprising. The book was reissued in 1971, and has been regularly reprinted since, suggesting the ongoing interest in the text as a relevant commentary on Western society and also as a historical document. Debord's thesis, for anyone brought up on a diet of Baudrillard and other postmodernists, is surprisingly familiar: he presents his thesis in proposition one: "The whole life of those societies in which modern conditions of production prevail presents itself as an immense accumulation of *spectacles*. All that was once directly lived has become mere representation" (1998: § 1, 12). This reads very much like the shift from the real to the simulation, although at this point it is not clear if Debord's spectacular society takes place in second- or third-order simulation. In fact, in the first chapter of *The Society of the Spectacle* we can see the importance of the book for Baudrillard's work. But is their work therefore identical? If not, what are the key differences? And why does Baudrillard end up critiquing Debord?

In the privileging of the human sense of sight, in the society of the spectacle, Debord argues that there is a distancing from the real world accessed most immediately through touch. Worse still, just because the spectacular can be seen, and seeing is a physiological and intellectual activity, it doesn't mean that the spectacle can be "altered" or inter- acted with: unlike touch, which suggests a Hegelian notion of work and transformation through physical labour, sight remains distant from the world. In this sense, the spectacle is the opposite of dialogue (1998: § 18, 17) and we can tie this in with Baudrillard's critique of the media in 1968 (touched upon in Chapter 2). This distance from the viewer and the viewed is clearly based upon a notion of perspectival space and the subject in a concrete world, separated from the holders of power. As such, Debord's notion of a whole society of the spectacle still remains structured in the classical sense of a division between the empowered and disempowered, a division which Baudrillard regards as collapsing and functioning in different ways in the hyperreal. Debord calls the spectacle a "self-portrait of power" (1998: § 24, 19) whereas in third-level simulation we no longer have the distance from the spec- tacle to stand back and see who is manipulating it as such: the situation is no longer that simple. Debord argues that the spectacle presents itself as the good, whereas Baudrillard regards the hyperreal as beyond questions of good and evil; both share notions of the performative, e.g. what works is "good" or what appears is "good", but as Debord's argu- ment unfolds it quickly becomes obvious that the society of the spectacle, while presenting itself in everyday life as good, is being critiqued by Debord as fundamentally bad or evil. Baudrillard seems to have a nostalgic desire for an existence that is not dominated by hyper- reality, based upon problematic notions of "primitive" societies, but he is less ready to make such massive ethical claims for either position. Put quite simply, as he does in *Simulations*, in hyperreality the subject is not actually "alienated" or "repressed" in the Marxist sense that we find in Debord. Baudrillard may not like every aspect of hyperreality, but it isn't a "fake" existence in the sense of the representation blurring with the real – it is another type of "reality", and that is how the subject experiences it. In a sense, Baudrillard takes the proposition from the first chapter of *The Society of the Spectacle* and radicalizes it in terms of structuralist/semiotic theory.

SUMMARY

Through two main examples, Watergate and Disneyland, we have seen what Baudrillard means by the hyperreal, where a kind of virtual reality is produced by models of what we want reality to be. Baudrillard argues that both of these examples "cover up" what is happening in the world, which has become both childish and duplicitous. We have seen such duplicity at work in the televisual Vietnam War, and with the links to Foucault's notion of "micro-powers". Baudrillard's analysis of war and film is related to his later comments on the Gulf War, where news produces a hyperreal war operating as a kind of testing ground for the concept of war itself. Baudrillard argues in relation to this that Foucault's and Debord's analyses are not radical enough, so he goes on to take their work to its limits with a semiotic twist.

SUMMARY

6

AMERICA AND POSTMODERNISM

This chapter reads one of Baudrillard's most infamous books – *America* – and shows how the actual place is important for many key postmodern concepts and issues. The modern and postmodern city space is analysed before moving to the desert and the seismic landscapes of California. Finally, the postmodern experience of the Bonaventure Hotel in LA concludes the chapter, with reference to the important American critic of postmodernism, Fredric Jameson.

THE PLACE OF POSTMODERNISM

In Chapter 5, we saw how events and locations, such as Watergate and Disneyland, reveal a shift into the hyperreal, and how in a wider sense the hyperreal can be thought of as a defining component of postmodernism, for example in thinking through the experiences and representations of the Vietnam and Gulf wars. It is no coincidence that these events and experiences are primarily American, either in terms of actual location, or involvement or perspective, since for Baudrillard America is *the* place of postmodernism. But the notion of American "place" in the singular is clearly problematized by a number of factors: the sheer size of the country, its immense cultural diversity, powerful historical and ideological notions, such as "the frontier", "the American dream" or "the world's police force", which construct notions of place that often override other concerns. Baudrillard's "reading" of America in many respects intersects with these factors: at times commenting upon them, at other times retheorizing them, but always with a local specificity deriving from the fact that his writings on America take the form of a travel narrative (in the texts *America* and *Cool Memories*). The travel narrative allows Baudrillard to present himself as both naïve and perceptive, someone just passing through and someone deeply involved with the culture being commented upon. This paradoxical position he takes *passing through* American culture, of necessity situates Baudrillard in the collapsed perspectival space of the hyperreal. In other words, he refuses to take the "distanced" position of a "superior" intellectual who can stand above and beyond the place, putting a distance between critic and experience. Other critics who attack him without taking this collapse into account, i.e. for being too naïve or too intellectual, have missed the point that both positions are operative at once.

CITIES OF THE EDGE

The modern space *par excellence* was the nineteenth- and early twentieth-century city: a place of rationality, industry, liberalism and progression. Modern cities were usually at the centre of huge empires, creating an opposition between city and countryside, urban and rural, or simply the contemporary and the *passé*. In the New World, the modern city came into its own: new building technologies enabled the "density" of office and housing space to increase exponentially, and cities of the future became present realities. This notion of the new is also important in the way that modern architecture developed: it wasn't so much a progression of old building techniques, but a break from and rejection of the past techniques. Henceforth, modern buildings, using glass and steel frames, would develop from this originary moment or resetting of history with the use of new technologies at year zero. In other words, the history of architecture would now start with the new ways of building as the past was denied and left behind. The language of the great modernist architects is utopian, based upon a fundamental belief in the rational cure of society's ills. In the new, functional relationship between the ways people worked and lived and the ways they could be housed, homes were now built like a machine, with repetitive similar housing "units" with light and air compared to the unhealthy workers' slums at the beginning of the Industrial

Revolution. Architects not only sought to realize solutions to age-old problems, such as poor-quality buildings, but also new problems, such as housing shortages that arose after the Industrial Revolution. Yet, for many people, this new functional urban space was something shocking, disorientating and deeply threatening, as great crowds of people were brought together for the first time on an unprecedented scale for urban living in a dense and charged atmosphere. Walter Benjamin asserts that "Fear, revulsion, and horror were the emotions which the big-city crowd aroused in those who first observed it" (1992: 170).

WALTER BENJAMIN

Benjamin (1892–1940) is probably one of the most famous theorists of modernity. His most well-known essays are "The Work of Art in the Age of Mechanical Reproduction" and "Theses on the Philosophy of History". Recently translated is Benjamin's great fragmentary work called *The Arcades Project*, an immense labyrinth of quotations, notes and essays. Benjamin links Marxist theory and Jewish messianism to create a unique series of insights into subjects such as art, history, literature, philosophy, photography and film. One of Benjamin's key authors/precursors is Charles Baudelaire (1821–1867), famous for his poetry, his theories of the *flâneur* (an idler or loafer, someone who strolls at random through the modern urban space), and his comments on the new city spaces of modernity.

Ironically, these crowds did not bring a feeling of community, but isolation and alienation: the city as a machine places the subject in its urban spaces just as he or she is positioned in the factory at the production line. Symbolically, the modern cities represented power: that of the economics that drove the new Americanized factories (with Taylorist principles and Fordist practice), and that of the empires such cities controlled. Modern cities were centres of power, projecting their economic, cultural and moral superiority across the world.

TAYLORISM AND FORDISM

Frederick Taylor's *Principles of Scientific Management*, published in 1911, was the culmination of many years spent collecting and analysing time and motion studies. These studies examined the ways in which workers moved and behaved when set various tasks, and were aimed at increasing productivity on the factory floor. The general application of Taylor's ideas became known, unsurprisingly, as Taylorism. The most famous shift in work practices took place with the opening of the production line in Highland Park, Detroit, by Henry Ford (1863–1947), the designer of the Model T Ford automobile. Ford directly applied Taylorist principles in a highly effective and successful way. However, the concept of Fordism involves extending the experiences and practices of the production line to other areas of social existence.

What makes a city postmodern? How different is Baudrillard's description of a city from, say, Baudelaire's? When he gets to New York, is Baudrillard describing a place, or merely writing firmly within a tradition, of Europeans visiting the New World, which they describe with the ideologies and landscapes and languages of the Old World? Baudrillard asks:

> Why do people live in New York? There is no relationship between them. Except for an inner electricity which results from the simple fact of their being crowded together. A magical sensation of contiguity and attraction for an artificial centrality. This is what makes it a self-attracting universe, which there is no reason to leave. There is no human reason to be here, except for the sheer ecstasy of being crowded together.
>
> (1988a: 15)

Commenting on Baudelaire, Walter Benjamin notes that the traffic of a big city involves the subject in "a series of shocks and collisions", the worst of which occur at busy and dangerous intersections where "... nervous impulses flow through him in rapid succession, like the energy from a battery" (1992: 171). Further, "Baudelaire speaks of a man who plunges into the crowd as into a reservoir of electric energy" (1992: 171). The key to this description of urban experience lies with the fact that in the mechanized world a single human gesture can trigger a sequence of results. Benjamin gives as examples the match, the telephone and the camera. These are technologies of detachment (humans no longer do all the physical work in the world), which return to haunt the subject, who becomes immersed in the triggered sequence or, to put this another way, the technologies of the city take on a life of their own which become shocking and frightening to the isolated individual, who wanders around the urban technological machine. Unlike the alienated dweller of a modern city, for Baudrillard, the postmodern city dweller enjoys – not fears – the "ecstasy" of the crowd, although it is only this "ecstasy" that gives them a reason for actually being physically present in the city. What does this signify? That the city is no longer the only place of work, that it no longer has the same sort of centralizing power that it once had, and that it no longer holds so much sway over the surrounding regions and smaller urban sites. Instead of people pouring into the modern city from the surrounding rural environment, people are now setting up living spaces in numerous locations that have the best of both worlds. In essence, the postmodern city is decentred and dispersed (Delany, 1994: 4). The experiences of the modern and postmodern city may therefore *appear* similar, but there has been a subtle shift in the *raison d'être* of the city space. Two examples can exemplify this subtle shift: that of geographical location and that of representation. Paul Delany argues that, as the modern centres are rendered less unique due to the dispersal of their functions or activities (such as being places of work and cultural production, e.g. television or the music industry), peripheral cities gain in vitality (1994: 4). These peripheral cities are usually cities of the edge, borderlands between land and sea, which "… illustrate the ecological principle that the greatest variety of life-forms will be found at the boundary between different habitats" (Delany, 1994: 19). Paradoxically, peripheral cities such as Vancouver or San Francisco are decentred and centred at the same time, because of the huge number of different cultures that collide there (but not necessarily to accumulate wealth and power for the colonial masters, but rather to make wealth or security for the postcolonial people who are often in the process of passing through). In *America*, Baudrillard describes New York and LA as being "at the centre of the world" (1988a: 23) – this "centre" is a paradoxical space, ironically revealed by Baudrillard by arguing *that two different locations occupy the centre at the same time*. The second example of the subtle shift in the *raison d'être* of the city space can be thought through in terms of representation, comparing film and television. Benjamin argues that, in the modern city, with its machine-like shocks and other processes, such as the new intensities of the factories and the mechanized transport systems, "... technology has subjected the human sensorium to a complex kind of training" (1999: 171):

> There came a day when a new and urgent need for stimuli was met by the film. In a film, perception in the form of shocks was established as a formal principle. That which determines the rhythm of production on a conveyor belt is the basis of the rhythm of reception in the film.
>
> (Benjamin, 1992: 171)

In other words, there is a circularity here between the machine-like existence of modern city dwellers preparing them for the experience of film, and the way in which film can train the city dweller (through new modes of perception) to function in a productive way as part of the industrial city-machine. How does this compare with Baudrillard's description of New York? In a moment of specific comparison, Baudrillard compares the European and American street. He argues that European streets only come alive periodically and sporadically in revolutionary upsurges – the rest of the time they are merely conduits for busy people. In America, however, Baudrillard uses the cliché that there are no comparative revolutionary moments to make the finer point that the streets are always revolutionary in their turbulence, energy and "cinematic" state (1988a: 18). A further comparison is made with the entire country, in the sense that change is prioritized, above all else, to make it a violent force (cities develop quickly, and are just as rapidly torn down and redeveloped, for example). But the source of that change – Baudrillard lists technology, racial differences and the media – is neither here nor there because the will to change is simply all-pervasive. The question is whether that change has a common goal (a modern telos) or merely exists for change itself, in a fragmented series of virtually random outcomes. Delany argues that the remote control is "the first and foremost postmodern tool" (1994: 5) – it is detached from the resulting events that its operation produces, but, more importantly in relation to change, flipping channels produces the feeling of infinite difference and the nightmare of ultimate similitude (that all the programmes claiming to be different are basically the same). Flipping through TV channels produces the effect of a richness of information, but ultimately it is an empty experience. Baudrillard's phrase to describe this experience is "autistic performance": "The New York marathon has become a sort of international symbol of such fetishistic performance, of the mania for an empty victory, the joy engendered by a feat that is of no consequence" (1988a: 20). The slogan which represents autistic performance is "I did it!" and Baudrillard compares its exclamation after the marathon with mountaineering and even the moon landing. The success of all these activities is preprogrammed by a society that knows in advance that it has the ability or technologies to achieve them. They are activities that appear to have a progressive aim, but in reality they have always already "been achieved": "Carrying out any kind of programme produces the same sense of futility that comes from doing anything merely to prove to yourself that you can do it ..." (1988a: 21).

Baudrillard's New York is a city of the mad set free, with the energy and electric "buzz" of the modern city taken to another level with its speeded-up non-teleological activity, or lack of a real goal. The city is approaching an apocalyptic state of speed, noise and overconsumption; with its "total electric light" and perpetual games, there is an artificiality that has broken away entirely from nature: the place is no longer in opposition to nature or its hinterlands. Baudrillard is fascinated by those who occupy this site, making him less a tourist or European academic, and more an anthropologist reaching or seeing a remote tribe for the first time:

> The terrifying diversity of faces, their strangeness, strained as they all are into unbelievable expressions. The masks old age or death conferred in archaic cultures are worn here by youngsters of twenty or twelve. But this reflects the city as a whole.
>
> (1988a: 14)

In such a vision of native death-masks and an accelerated culture, Baudrillard reads New York almost as a Surrealist painting or text; his vision of clouds filling people's heads or coming out of their eyes conflates architecture and human subject, compresses the verticality and horizontality of skyscraper and sky with that of the subject and the street. But the effect isn't one of claustrophobia – the opposite is the case. Using the cliché of the sickly European sky compared to the immensity of the North American sky, Baudrillard adds another factor: the reflection of the city and its environment from the glass skyscrapers. However, this hyperreal expansion of space through the reflection of huge skyscrapers is already obsolete. Instead, the post-modern city *par excellence* will be the horizontal space of Los Angeles, where cities expand by consuming more and more of the surrounding land in a kind of self-replication process, before the city disappears altogether: "New York is the final fling of this baroque verticality, this centrifugal excentricity, before the horizontal dismantling arrives, and the subterranean implosion that will follow" (1988a: 22).

PARIS, TEXAS – OR – THE DESERT

In Wim Wenders' film *Paris, Texas*, a man called Travis walks out of the American desert and into a bar, where he eventually collapses from exhaustion. The desert appears to have erased his memory to such an extent that he has forgotten how to speak. After Travis is rescued by his brother, painful memories from the past are most vividly recalled by some home movies; Travis eventually begins to speak again as he inter-acts with his son and begins the search for his lost wife. The film, which is structured by division and journeys, ends with an ambiguous reconciliation between mother and child, with Travis still on the road, still in a state of perpetual movement. The desert and the road movie – two of the most powerful devices of American cinema and symbols of the American way of life because of the ways in which American society is constantly reinventing itself, removing the traces of what has been constructed for something new, always moving on in time and space. *Paris, Texas*, as the name suggests, plays on the divisions and differences between New and Old Worlds, both in the sense of America and Europe, and new life/old life in more personal or indi-vidual terms. The juxtaposition of such dissimilar places provides the movie with a tension, between questions of origin(s) and ways of starting again, a perpetual newness to erase the pains of the past. Paradoxically, the truly ancient desert landscapes of the West are also the "newest" places in postmodern America.

Baudrillard's American deserts are cinematic before the invention of cinema and semiotic before the invention of human sign-systems.

SEMIOTICS

Semiotics can be thought of as a "science of signs" (see "structuralism" : p. 15). While it is an approach that has parallels with structuralism, the main difference is that *semioticians search for the logical rules or laws of signs and sign-systems*. Semiotics is therefore a more formal and "purist" approach. However, for all its scientific pretensions, for example with the analysis and modelling of communication systems, it would be more accurate to think of semiotics as a "pseudo-science" or theory. Apart from the importance of Ferdinand de Saussure (1857–1913), one of the "founding fathers" of semiotics was Charles Sanders Peirce (1839–1914), who equated logic with the science of signs (see Hawkes, 1977: 126). One of the key components of Peirce's system is that of the triad of signs called the icon, index and symbol. The icon is a sign that bears a similarity to the object (such as a painting), an index is a sign that has a material relationship with the object (such as smoke signifying fire), and a symbol has an *arbitrary* relationship with the object (the symbolic sign, in other words, is constructed through a cultural system).

It is important, however, not to confuse them with other deserts, other landscapes:

> The American desert is an extraordinary piece of drama, though in no sense is it theatrical like an Alpine landscape, nor sentimental like the forest or the countryside. Nor eroded and monotonous like the sub-lunar Australian desert. Nor mystical, like the deserts of Islam. It is purely, geologically dramatic, bringing together the sharpest, most ductile shapes with the gentlest, most lascivious underwater forms – the whole metamorphism of the earth's crust is present in synthesis, in a miraculous abridged version.
>
> (1988a: 69)

Baudrillard is careful to distinguish between landscapes here, because he wishes to reveal the difference between those deserts which have entered mythology or theology through centuries of human cartography and shifts in imperial or colonial power (like the deserts in Ondaatje's *The English Patient*), and those deserts where the human subject is merely an actor or player in a pre-existing scene. Another way of thinking through the latter is with reference to the opening shot in Wenders' *Paris, Texas*, where the camera looks down on Travis from the perspective of an eagle: the desert looks at Travis before Travis looks at the desert. The desert pre-exists man geologically, but it also pre-exists man semiotically – that is to say, nature isn't presented in *America* as some blind force, or a force directed by God; rather it is a geological sign-system:

> Geological – and hence metaphysical – monumentality, by contrast with the physical altitude of ordinary landscapes. Upturned relief patterns, sculpted out by wind, water, and ice ... The very idea of the millions and hundreds of millions of years that were needed peacefully to ravage the surface of the earth here is a perverse one, since it brings with it an awareness of signs originating, long before man appeared, in a sort of pact of wear and erosion struck between the elements.
>
> (1988: 3)

Condensed in this description of the Grand Canyon is a vision of the American landscape as surpassing the European norm; not in terms of a European Romantic sublime (a way of perceiving the landscape prevalent in the nineteenth century), but in terms of the monumentality of the landscape – a landscape constructed on a grand scale and left as a reminder that humanity is just one in a series of signifying systems. But there is something else going on here and throughout the text: Baudrillard is critiquing the nature/culture binary opposition through which such sublime landscapes are usually interpreted. In his account, nature is already cultural and culture has to take into account other alien signifying systems (which we will see later as relating to Baudrillard's conception of the symbolic). How is this critique of the nature/culture binary opposition possible? And why does it need to be performed in the first place?

We can think of the modern, in a crude sense, as the instrumental manipulation of nature for cultural or technological aims. Nature is something that needs to be left behind or overpowered, as the great industrial and urbanization programmes go hand in hand towards building a new world that has thoroughly broken with the past. However, postmodernism reincorporates the past into itself as a way of attempting to construct an aesthetically "richer" experience, especially – or more obviously – in the realm of architecture. That is not to say, however, that modernism (see page 28) cannot itself be one of the historical elements that postmodernism employs. Examples of this "reincorporation" include the Museum of Contemporary Art in Los Angeles, a building of steel and brick that contains a huge curved Palladian window, and the Clore Gallery in London, which is the extension to the Tate Gallery. With the Clore, the classicism of the Tate is reflected in the pergola, pool and trellis (see Jencks, 1987: 165 for photographs).

Put even more simply, the machine aesthetic rejects the natural, organic past, while postmodernism welcomes it. Some examples of anthropomorphic (resembling the human form) architecture and the construction of postmodern space should illuminate the ways in which "nature" is reworked and reintroduced. Charles Jencks notes how, with the work of architects such as Minoru Takeyama and Kazumasa Yamashita, images of the body are used in a completely unsubtle way; Takeyama's *Beverly Tom Hotel* (1973–1974) uses phallic imagery both inside and outside the building and Yamashita's *Face House* (1974) is, reductively, nothing but a boxy face. More subtle, however, is the boundary-blurring work of architect Michael Graves, who deconstructs the thresholds of architecture: windows, doorways and overall profiles. The subject is slowed down in his or her transition from interior to exterior (or vice versa) by the interest generated and the new pleasures of these spaces, and thus experiences the natural elements that are dramatized by such an architecture (Jencks, 1987: 117). Finally, in a wider sense, postmodern space overall historicizes itself, but also creates blurred boundaries both internally and externally, unlike the uniform space of the modern. Jencks argues that postmodern space is not really organic, but "... an elaboration of the Cartesian grid ..." or system of mental mapping (1987: 118). This summary is correct because, while postmodernism can incorporate or structure itself partially via the organic, such a process is part of a more complex package of ideas and sources. The moderns may have had a notion of a pure nature/culture opposition. By blurring the boundaries between nature/culture, postmodernism is doing more than allowing organic elements "into" its structures; it is suggesting that in some ways the organic already exists in the cultural and that the cultural is already organic. Thus the *evolution* of postmodern architecture instead of the *revolutions* of the modern.

The impossible binary nature/culture was explored most famously by the structuralist anthropologist Claude Lévi-Strauss. In an essay called "Structure, Sign and Play in the Discourse of the Human Sciences", Jacques Derrida notes how the structuralist analysis of the incest prohibition led to the "scandal" of the critique of the nature/culture binary: "The incest prohibition is universal; in this sense one could call it natural. But it is also a prohibition, a system of norms and interdicts; in this sense one could call it cultural" (1978: 283). The incest scandal is something which should be either generated by cultural law or by natural law; instead, it is outside of (or precedes) both systems because it cannot be "contained" by either. Derrida argues that such a problematic binary is impossible to think through in philosophy, while being something that simultaneously grounds philosophy. He concludes that such binaries either need intense investigation, or they are used as "tools" to interrogate thought systems from within. This brings us back to Baudrillard in the desert with his own critique of the nature/culture binary. Baudrillard uses the discourse of travel writing and of commenting on the great American cities, roads and landscape, not as a way of being just one more in a long line of European commentators, but as a way of both retaining the discourse while critiquing its assumptions. The desert becomes for Baudrillard what Rodolphe Gasché calls an "infrastructure"; that is to say, something which generates signifying systems but then disappears when we try and pin it down (see Gasché, 1986).

Baudrillard's travel narrative, thought of in this more philosophical way, is both postmodern performance and critical commentary. His travel narrative, unlike the modern Europeans', is non-teleological; it is "... the conception of a trip without any objective ..." (1988a: 9). The form of American culture that is found in the West is seismic: "a fractal, interstitial culture, born of a rift with the Old World, a tactile, fragile, mobile, superficial culture ..." (1988a: 10). "Superficial" is meant in the sense of surfaces replacing the old depth-models of modernity (the "inner" compared to "surface" knowledge), and the generation of a "seismic" model here allows not only for the shifting of surfaces, but also the potential of their collision, disruption and apocalyptic destruction at the same time as they are consumed or lived as present-day utopias. As Baudrillard says, this is the land of the "Just as it is", which means that the seismic possibilities are ignored (1988a: 28). The seismic desert landscape is a "primal scene" from which, and through which, the culture, politics and sexuality of America must be read. The desert is already cinematic: "The desert you pass through is like the set of a Western, the city a screen of signs and formulas" (1988a: 56). Yet, like a television set left on in an empty room, nobody is watching the deserts for their semiotic significance (see Lane, 1999). Baudrillard states that:

> My hunting grounds are the deserts, the mountains, Los Angeles, the freeways, the Safeways, the ghost towns, or the downtowns, not lectures at the university. I know the deserts, their deserts, better than they do, since they turn their backs on their own space as the Greeks turned their backs on the sea, and I get to know more about the concrete, social life of America from the desert than I ever would from official or intellectual gatherings.
>
> (1988a: 63)

The desert is not held in opposition to the cities or to culture in general; rather they reveal that third-order simulation generates a cultural mirage, which presumably will eventually disappear to leave only the desert. The desert is thus a background, a past and future possibility, a vision that pervades the postmodern American culture. Baudrillard calls the deserts "our mythic operator", which is to say that the deserts are symbolic for an infinite number of cultural formations, like the alien "sea" in Stanislaw Lem's *Solaris*, but, unlike a computer-generated image based on a series of mathematical formulae, when the formation has disappeared the desert is still physically present. In some ways, postmodern cities can be compared with the deserts: their constant reinvention and spatial drift is analogous to the shifting sands and erasure of geological formations, but cities are also desiring machines (places where the system of needs are generated), whereas the desert precedes desire even as it still critiques the nature/culture binary by being a potential signifying system prior to human existence: "... the desert is simply that: an ecstatic critique of culture, an ecstatic form of disappearance" (1988a: 5).

THE BONAVENTURE HOTEL

With the pre-eminence of the advanced technologies of Silicon Valley, the simulations that are Disneyland and Hollywood, and the great Los Angeles decentred urban sprawl itself, California appears to be post-modern through and through. How does the subject experience this postmodernity? How do people interact with, or find themselves in, this new space for living in? In *The Dismemberment of Orpheus* (1982), Ihab Hassan constructed a now widely referred to and complex list, which enables us to compare and contrast the differences between modernism and postmodernism. This list can be examined not just for its intellectual content, but also its *experiential* aspect, in that it describes the ways we experience these two worlds:

Modernism	Postmodernism
Romanticism/Symbolism	'Pataphysics/Dadaism
Form (conjunctive/closed)	Antiform (disjunctive, open)
Purpose	Play
Design	Chance
Hierarchy	Anarchy
Mastery/Logos	Exhaustion/Silence
Art Object/Finished Work	Process/Performance/Happening
Distance	Participation
Creation/Totalization	Decreation/Deconstruction
Synthesis	Antithesis
Presence	Absence
Centring	Dispersal
Genre/Boundary	Text/Intertext
Paradigm	Syntagm
Hypotaxis	Parataxis
Metaphor	Metonymy
Selection	Combination
Root/Depth	Rhizome/Surface
Interpretation/Reading	Against Interpretation/Misreading
Signified	Signifier
Lisible (Readerly)	*Scriptible* (Writerly)
Narrative/*Grand Histoire*	Anti-narrative/*Petit Histoire*
Master Code	Idiolect
Symptom	Desire
Genital/Phallic	Polymorphous/Androgynous
Paranoia	Schizophrenia
Origin/Cause	Difference–Différance/Trace
Metaphysics	Irony
Determinacy	Indeterminacy
Transcendence	Immanence

(Hassan, 1982: 267–268)

We have seen with New York how the city generates the potential anarchy of the crowd charged with desire, ranging the streets in a permanent state of performance; we have also seen how the post-modern city is decentred and dispersed through a series of "peripheral" city-sites replacing the singular modern centre. The desert has been theorized as a place of exhaustion and potential: it is a kind of textual surface which can be remoulded in an infinite variety of shifting, temporary forms which, as Baudrillard argues, will ultimately collapse. But what about postmodern buildings themselves, situated as they are as a kind of midpoint between desert and city, between the solitary individual and the crowd? One of the most theorized postmodern buildings is the Bonaventure Hotel in Los Angeles, which Baudrillard theorizes as ludic and hallucinogenic, while Fredric Jameson empha-sizes the disjunctive nature of the experience of simply moving through the building; the building itself, to refer to Hassan's list, is against interpretation and open always to misreading.

One of the key factors in the Bonaventure experience is the way in which the building fails to interact with the local city environment: physically, there is no singular grand entrance; visually, with five huge towers of mirror-plate glass, the city is thrown back upon itself. The hotel, cut off in this way from the city, isn't asserting its difference or superiority (such as might be found in the new architectural languages of modernism as modernist buildings were placed violently in the traditional urban space); instead, the Bonaventure is a miniature city, holistic in its perfect reproduction of all of the city utilities and spaces (Baudrillard, 1988a: 60). Jameson argues that the modernist disjunc-tion between building and city was "... violent, visible and had a very real symbolic significance", leading to the expected transformation of the degraded city fabric into the utopian space of the modern (1998: 12–13). However, the Bonaventure has no such ideals or purpose; its reflection of the city suggests an acceptance of the surrounding space and in this sense I would argue that it *does* have an interface at the level of the image and the spectacle.

As the subject moves into the building there is instant confusion because he or she appears to be in the middle of an undefined space, needing to travel in a number of directions to find the check-in desk, for example. Baudrillard notes that one "... cannot fathom out its internal space, but it has no mystery" (1988a: 60). This latter is impor-tant, because it makes the experience for him "empty", lacking in actual concrete content: the building is a "box of spatio-temporal tricks" (1988a: 59). This is hyperreal architecture, a series of spatio-temporal simulations, which means that the subject finds himself or herself in the wrong place at the right time, or the right place at the wrong time; these tricks therefore work primarily through disorientation, even at the level of just getting in the building:

> The entryways of the Bonaventure are, as it were, lateral and rather backdoor affairs: the gardens in the back admit you to the sixth floor of the towers, and even there you must walk down one flight to find the elevator by which you gain access to the lobby. Meanwhile, what one is still tempted to think of as the front entry, on Figueroa, admits you, baggage and all, onto the second-storey balcony, from which you must take an escalator down to the main registration desk.
>
> (Jameson, 1998: 12)

Even though the building has vertical components, it is structured like a palimpsest – a series of layers – which the subject has to negotiate as if in a labyrinth (see Lane, 1993). These layers, through being interconnected in "illogical" ways, disrupt the relationship between horizontal and vertical, which allows us to perceive volume:

> ... if it seemed to you before that the suppression of depth observable in post-modern painting or literature would necessarily be difficult to achieve in architecture itself, perhaps you may now be willing to see this bewildering immersion as its formal equivalent in the new medium.
>
> (Jameson, 1998: 14)

Jameson argues that human beings have not yet evolved the perceptual equipment needed to deal with such a hyperspace as he calls it. I would argue that, nearly two decades on, with the advent of virtual-reality technologies and even the hypertext links in standard Web-page use (where the user clicks on a highlighted bit of text and jumps to another Web site automatically), this hyperspace is no longer quite as problematic. The task of actually moving around the Bonaventure building, with all its playful disruptions and disappointments, its disorienting techniques and attacks on cognitive mapping skills, becomes analogous to the computer game, which in itself uses the notion of "levels" to mean more of the same but slightly more difficult, rather than referring to the modern verticality of the imposing skyscrapers that function far more two-dimensionally.

Is the Bonaventure utopia achieved? Is this labyrinthine, but self-enclosed and safe, miniature city the urban environment perfected, either in terms of its game-playing potential or with the fact that its only dangers seem to be a slight headache in getting from an entrance to the hotel check-in desk? The building is a residential shopping mall where the insane are definitely kept out (hotel security in this sense having *already* replaced the official police force, who fail to maintain law and order in the city space itself). But this sanitized environment is, for Baudrillard, a sign of death: utopia achieved is a negation of the struggle, of the processes of becoming; it is what Oswald Spengler in *The Decline of the West* (1926) called *the become* or the *hard-set*. America begs this question: What do you do when everything is available ...? (Baudrillard, 1988a: 30). The perfection of society is also its end. However, this seems to contradict the ludic nature of buildings like the Bonaventure, the fact that the games played in them *are* their "meaning", so to speak. Also, the new spaces and experiences of post-modernity are not necessarily as sanitized as Baudrillard makes out. Postmodern America produces non-territorial weapons; that is to say, weapons which physically rain down on an enemy, but electronically bombard the entire world through television (Baudrillard, 1988a: 49). Jameson takes this notion further, making a direct link between the new perceptual spaces of postmodern buildings and their analogue: postmodern warfare. With the Vietnam War, the grand narratives of the war correspondent could no longer function, since the action was schizophrenic (taking place "on the ground" and in a virtual reality of fake body-counts and television bulletins), the nationalistic intentions and theories suspect (the domino theory which would lead to the destruction of the West by Communist regimes if Vietnam fell), and the combatants high on a range of recreational drugs as a way of coping with the insane demands placed upon them. For Jameson, the problem becomes one of finding a new discourse actually to write about this experience, connecting thereby what is happening in the sanitized world of the Bonaventure and other such buildings with the realm of the postmodern war; this discourse is found in Vietnam War journalist Michael Herr's book *Dispatches*:

The extraordinary linguistic innovations of this work may be considered post-modern in the eclectic way in which its language impersonally fuses a whole range of contemporary collective idiolects, most notably rock language and black language, but the fusion is dictated by problems of content. This first terrible postmodernist war cannot be recounted in any of the traditional paradigms of the war novel or movie – indeed, that breakdown of all previous narrative paradigms is, along with the breakdown of any shared experience, among the principal subjects of the book and may be said to open up the place of a whole new reflexivity.

(Jameson, 1998: 16)

The ways in which Herr constructs his hallucinogenic account of the war through "collective idiolects" – that is, languages or discourses drawn from popular culture – is analogous to the ways in which the Bonaventure constructs its architectural codes out of the American architectural vernacular (everyday normal experiences, such as checking in at a "normal" hotel, which are then totally disrupted). Like the construction of a truly great American literature from the vernacular/idioloects, for example, with Mark Twain's *The Adventures of Huckleberry Finn*, postmodern architecture holds "utopia achieved" in tension with "apocalypse now" – they are both sides of the same coin.

SUMMARY

In this chapter we have seen how America is the place of postmodernism for Baudrillard. Baudrillard's semiotic conception of the American desert enables us to understand how he theorizes the modernist and postmodernist city-spaces and experiences. We have seen that the decentred postmodern city incorporates the organic and the evolutionary, whereas the modernist city rejected nature and was a revolutionary space. With examples such as the postmodern experience of the Bonaventure Hotel in Los Angeles, and the movement and disorientation of "postmodern" war, we have seen how Baudrillard's work relates to other critical theorists such as Fredric Jameson.

7

WRITING STRATEGIES

Postmodern performance

In this concluding chapter Baudrillard's writing strategies are examined as a way of addressing a whole host of recurring themes and concepts in his work. In particular, it examines the way in which Baudrillard's postmodern writings are seen as performance pieces with no real content and why this should be so, given Baudrillard's philosophical and theoretical backgrounds. The chapter examines terrorism, nihilism, and Baudrillard's contradictory position as critic or defender of postmodernism.

SIMUVAC

There is a scene in the American postmodern novelist Don DeLillo's *White Noise* where the residents of a small Middle American town are simulating a major disaster in preparation for the "real" thing. The irony in this is that the "real" has already occurred with the "toxic airborne event". The protagonist asks: "Are you people sure you're ready for a simulation? You may want to wait for one more massive spill. Get your timing down" (1986: 204). The reaction to the toxic airborne event has been chaotic, random, terrible, whereas the simulation is ordered, organized and peaceful. The private consulting firm that operates the simulated evacuation stress the importance of a "logic" revealed to be based upon myth: "The more we rehearse disaster, the safer we'll be from the real thing. Life seems to work that way, doesn't it?" (1986: 205). Using the example of forgetting to take an umbrella to work and that being the day that it rains, the firm's representatives suggests that this "mechanism" will be "employed" among others, implying a saturation of the "real" with the simulation, until the "real" is negated or neutralized (in other words, turned into the hyperreal). *White Noise* is a novel saturated with the fear of the "real" irrupting into the hyperreal (such as a real disaster interrupting the simulation), and the hyperreal irrupting into the "real" (such as the protagonist's obsession with death meaning something in the real world). Events are only ever thought about in relation to or through media response and representation, or in terms of what was happening in the world of the media at the time (e.g. the death of JFK). There is a constant teasing-out of any hint of *inauthenticity*, a constant bantering between characters about the disjunction between information overload and the feeling that nothing about the world, about being in the world, is known. At the same time, various university professors lurk around the campus town, performing semiotic analyses of popular culture, supermarkets and American history. *White Noise* is perhaps the book critics would have liked to have seen instead of Baudrillard's *America*, the former not containing so many of the Eurocentric stereotypes of the latter, while still covering much of the same cultural territory. One of the problems with Baudrillard's *America* (and other works) is that it does not have the fall-back position of a DeLillo novel; that is to say, however "accurate" DeLillo's descriptions of postmodern American society may be, they are essentially categorized as "fiction" and can therefore be laughed with or at, rejected, accepted and so on, safe in the knowledge that they can be put down and the "real" non-fictional world returned to. Baudrillard, after *Symbolic Exchange and Death*, roughly speaking, refuses to make such a fine distinction between fiction and documentary, or fiction and academic text.

TERRORISM

The protagonist in Don DeLillo's *Mao II* (1992) argues that as the power and efficacy of novels to affect the "inner life" of a culture wanes, that of terrorism increases: "Now bomb-makers and gunmen have taken that territory. They make raids on human consciousness. What writers used to do before we were all incorporated" (1992: 41).

The notion of terrorist "territory" is important to Baudrillard in this sense: it is a conceptual territory. In *Simulacra and Simulation*, the argument runs that it is impossible to stage an illusion because the real has disappeared. Go and hold a fake hold-up, Baudrillard suggests, with fake weapons, a hostage and as much performance close to the "real" thing as possible. Then look at the consequences:

> ... you won't succeed: the web of artificial signs will be inextricably mixed up with real elements (a police officer will really shoot on sight; a bank customer will faint and die of a heart attack; they will really turn the phoney ransom over to you) in brief, you will unwittingly find yourself immediately in the real, one of whose functions is precisely to devour every attempt at simulation ...
>
> (1983b:39)

Simulation is theorized as being more threatening to the established order (who construct the acceptable legalized "real") precisely because it can reveal that the "real" of law and order is a simulation in the first place. The argument runs that a "simulated" hold-up will be punished for either falling short of success or being too successful, but never for being a simulation itself. The implications, according to Baudrillard, are that "law and order" belong to second-order simulation (the "real" and the "representation" blur into one another), whereas the simulation event "itself" belongs to third-order simulation or the hyperreal (there is nothing to compare it with). But, to go beyond our earlier analysis of these simulation categories, the issue now becomes that if simulation cannot be verified, neither can the real. Terrorist activity impacts upon society in a straightforward way because it has become a preprogrammed event, which will be analysed and presented by the media according to an unfolding of expected sequences, and so on. Baudrillard asserts, however, that this does not mean that such activity has been neutralized; if anything, the hyperreality of the terrorist "attack" becomes even more frightening in its dispersal and reoccurrence or, to put it another way, in its effect, which always takes place elsewhere (in the mode or processes of representation). Terrorist activity tests the limits of society, of its institutions of power and the way in which such institutions are located conceptually. In *Fatal Strategies*, the terrorists and the hostages have become "unnamable"; that is to say, they exist in a homogeneous society (the perfection of "utopia achieved") which it is their function to interrupt, re-code, redirect. The hyperreality of postmodernism is beyond good and evil: the work of the terrorist is to return society to the world of ethical structures and events. But this is a fantasy, an impossibility, since the territory of terrorism is no longer located at the margins of society, a fracturing or insertion point:

> We speak of "terrorist space": airports, embassies, fractile zones, non-territorial zones. The embassy is the infinitesimal space in which a whole country can be taken hostage. The plane, with its passengers, is a parcel of land, a wandering molecule of enemy territory, and therefore almost no longer a territory, therefore almost a hostage already, since to take something hostage is to tear it from its territory and revert it to the equilibrium of terror. Today this terror is our normal, silent condition everywhere ...
>
> (1990b: 38)

The interconnectedness of contemporary society – where every occurrence must have a cause (Butler, 1999: 90) – leads to an overdetermined society that takes the notion of "security" to the limit, a kind of oversaturation of security. From this position, however, the smallest, most random upsetting of the overdetermined status quo becomes incredibly frightening, like the snapping of a small branch in a forest at night. Where did the noise come from? Who caused it? Who is out there? Where exactly are they? How big are they? The questions and perceived threats escalate by the moment. The paradox for Baudrillard is that terrorism takes advantage of this situation (indeed, contemporary terrorism is structured along these lines) and is neutralized by it (because society is detached, deterritorialized, "managed" from the extraterritorial, extraplanetary space, held hostage under nuclear threat in its entirety).

The subject now perceived as existing via the blackmail of the nuclear society, internalized via the "blackmail" of the body, its economies, and those of the family, leads to the question of where Baudrillard as subject(ed) situates himself in relation to this and other visions of the world. His writing has been condemned as too performative (and therefore not analytical enough, or philosophical, sociological, psychological ... enough) and as being simply a manifestation of some kind of postmodern nihilism, situated like the hyperreal in a Nietzschean space beyond good and evil. The question becomes: Who, and where, is Baudrillard in his texts?

NIHILISM

In a short essay on nihilism in *Simulacra and Simulation*, Baudrillard writes "I am a nihilist" (1994a: 160). This statement, so straightforward and certain, is deconstructed by the text that produces it.

NIHILISM

Nihilism is an extreme form of rejection: of authority, institutions, systems of belief (especially religious beliefs) and value. Nihilism can also be defined as a revolutionary destruction for its own sake and therefore the practice or promulgation of terrorism (*Collins English Dictionary*). To say "I am a nihilist" is to form a series of affiliations, intellectually the strongest being with the work of German philosopher Friedrich Nietzsche (1844–1900), who infamously asserts in his texts that "God is dead". It is Nietzsche who performed one of the most sustained analyses of belief systems as being *themselves* nihilistic.

Baudrillard's statement can be summarized thus: "If nihilism is 'x', then I am a nihilist." But this only temporarily stabilizes what it means to be a nihilist in the postmodern world, where nihilism has been "entirely realized" (1994a: 159) and is simultaneously "impossible" (1994a: 161). The accusation that Baudrillard is ultimately a nihilist postmodernist writer (rather than a more serious academic person) must be brought into contact with this short essay in *Simulacra and Simulation*, to decide if it is possible to locate the speaking voice of Baudrillard's texts in such a straightforward way and accuse the voice/subject/Baudrillard of being a certain negative type of writer.

When we think of the rejection of "higher values" in nihilism, for example the denial of a god or a religious system, then we are referring to a *reactive nihilism* – the domination of "higher values" is reacted against. But there is another position or perspective that precedes this: that the "higher values" in saying that they are superior to life itself (the supersensuous versus the sensuous), depreciate or negate life (Deleuze, 1983: 147). This is called *negative nihilism*. Deleuze notes that "… [with negative nihilism] essence was opposed to appearance, life was turned into an appearance. Now [with reactive nihilism] essence is denied but appearance is retained: everything is merely appearance ..." (1983: 148). We can translate this as saying that with negative nihilism the "essence" of human beings, such as the soul or the spirit, is deemed real, while the "appearances", or how the world appears to a being (see Nehamas, 1985: 45), are deemed false and degraded. With reactive nihilism, the "essences" are denied, such as the holy spirit in man, and all we have are the "appearances" or perspectives upon the world. Meaning in the reactively nihilistic world is generated by humanity, not some being who precedes or transcends humanity. For Baudrillard, postmodernity is about the play of "appearances" and the destruction of symbolic meaning (1994a: 160). Baudrillard argues that in the post-modern world we are involved in the empty and meaningless play of the media ("play" as in chance, and "play" as in the playback of a prere-corded piece of information, music or software). Baudrillard calls the play of the media a "transparency", because all values become ulti-mately "indifferent forms". Think of the ways in which advertising absorbs and regurgitates the seemingly radical forms of the avant-garde, thus a piece of art that attempts to challenge the whole system of aesthetics can be used to advertise some gizmo or haircare product on television. A transparent system is one where the avant-garde is neutralized as a style, fashion or trend in advance, which means that there is no point in even trying to artistically challenge any system. How does the theorist operate or write within this transparency? Baudrillard suggests that critical analysis has itself become uncertain and open to chance (1994a: 161). And in *this* sense, nihilism cannot exist any more because it is still a solidified theory or critical analysis of existence.

"I am a nihilist" says the narrative voice of "On Nihilism". But is the voice a narrator or protagonist? Someone outside of, or above post-modernism ... or inside, writing about postmodernism through postmodernism? "I am a nihilist", says the voice, but only if nihilism is defined in certain ways: first, if it is nihilistic to see "the masses" as being caught up in another paradoxical notion, that of an accelerated inertia, and to privilege this paradoxical point in its analysis; and second, if it is nihilistic to be obsessed with the mode of the destruc-tion or disappearance of meaning (1994a: 162). But to be nihilistic with these provisos is not to be nostalgic; instead, there is a more profound melancholia behind the nostalgia that one finds in figures such as Walter Benjamin, who lamented the destruction of meaning in the modern world of Nazism and war. Baudrillard's persona at this point identifies deeply with this melancholia.

WRITING/READING STRATEGIES

How do we deal with the fact that Baudrillard's writing career can be thought of as an extended attack upon the hyperreal and the loss of the symbolic, while he himself is considered a defender of the post-modern or a postmodern nihilist? Throughout this text there has been the suggestion that many of the reactions to Baudrillard have been to do with his style of writing. Thus, when Christopher Norris calls Baudrillard a "... cult figure on the current 'postmodernist' scene, and purveyor of some of the silliest ideas yet to gain a hearing among disciples of French intellectual fashion" (1992: 11), there is a delib-erate emphasis on the stylistic aspects of his work. Baudrillard is condemned because he is a "cult figure" and his followers are condemned as not being real thinkers, but merely people who follow the latest intellectual "fashion" (worse still, from an English perspec-tive, it is "French" fashion). Yet Baudrillard is partly to blame for this travesty, because he has situated himself as an intellectual precisely at the level of style or fashion as a way of writing at the limits of the hyperreal. As Bryan Turner notes, books like *America* and *Cool Memories* "... are offensive to academics, especially serious academics like Callinicos and Kellner [who both perform strong critiques of Baudrillard], because they are politically uncommitted, whimsical, and depthless" (Rojek and Turner, 1993: 152). But, unlike Norris, Turner is not saying this as a way of condemning such texts; rather he is describing them *as* writing strategies. If we return to the text *America* discussed in Chapter 3, we can think of its form as travel-narrative and the parallels with the "American" road movie. But another metaphor can be used to describe Baudrillard's style – that of "cruising". As Turner notes, "A cruise is a trip or voyage typically undertaken for pleasure; it is a trivial exercise ... Cruising is pointless, aimless and unproductive. It leaves no residue, no evidence, no archive. It does not intend to interpret; it is post-anthropological" (Rojek and Turner, 1993: 153). Baudrillard doesn't simply analyse cultural forms, but explores them through a doubling of those forms: his texts are cultural events that partake of the structures of postmodernity. Turner sees a parallel with the restlessness of 1960s American writing (see also Lane, 1999):

> Both Baudrillard and Kerouac are involved in a "reading" of the society through the flashing vision of American culture as a seen [sic] through the car screen, the rear mirror or the subway. The car screen and the TV screen have a number of things in common. The passenger, like the viewer, is passive, indifferent, entertained and perhaps over-stimulated by the flashing trivia of the landscape and scene.
>
> (Rojek and Turner, 1993: 153)

But how are we, as readers, supposed to make sense of this journey? Presumably (to adopt the position of the "serious" reader) we have come to Baudrillard's work not as we would a television programme or a novel, but expecting some intellectual content? Perhaps reading Baudrillard is for some already not a problem because they are so involved in the experiential nature of their own postmodern world(s)? Or perhaps others may have to develop particular reading strategies to cope with the writing strategies being used? Mike Gane suggests that as a "theoretical extremist" Baudrillard takes his ideas to their logical limits, but that the reader then needs some "basic protocols" or rules to respond to and make sense of the resulting work. Reading Baudrillard is broken down into a number of phases: first a phase where the reader is seduced into a suspension of his or her critical faculties as they drift in the "flow" of Baudrillard's work; and second, an abrupt reversal of this phase as the reader becomes hypercritical of Baudrillard's work, finally, a more balanced series of readings are produced out of the extremities of these positions (Gane, 1991: 7–10). Gane regards phases one and two as a kind of potentially self-destructive "delirium", his position being reminiscent of the fears that often surround(ed) Nietzsche's work (the "madness" is somehow contagious). The notion of a more balanced series of readings doesn't really explain why the reader had to become delirious in the first place: while Gane defends Baudrillard from the many attacks upon his work, particularly from Marxist thinkers, the notion of a delirious reading could have been productively expanded to tie in with the radicality of the work under discussion.

Returning to Turner's analysis of Baudrillard's style, we can look more closely at the parallels between text and hyperreality being "described". In his analysis of the postmodern "cruising" text, Turner suggests four technical components:

1   priority of style/form, where content and matter are diversions;
2   any "message" is constructed via repetition leading to an "explosion of meaning";
3   literary hyperbole (exaggeration used for effect) becomes analogous to hyperreality;
4   the sequential order of the text (linear progression) replaced by self-contained segments, which can be read in any order.
(modified from Rojek and Turner, 1993: 155)

This list, or one with minor modifications, can be used as a guide to virtually all of the texts produced after *Symbolic Exchange and Death*, although the division between serious (early)/playful (later) works should not blind us to the fact that Baudrillard addresses a series of related issues across his entire oeuvre. In his postmodern style, Baudrillard dislocates the traditional location of meaning in an analytical text, but that *does not* lead to a "meaningless" text that has nothing to say.

ENDING WITH POSTMODERNISM

The lack or rejection of closure was once one of the most celebrated facets of postmodernism: openness, continual play, plurality of perspectives and the endless chance to produce something radically new. But how does postmodernism account for or deal with events on a vast historical scale, such as the "Big Bang" or "the millennium"? With the latter, competing disaster theories proliferate and circulate among the media, from messianic and apocalyptic predictions of a spiritual type, to the banal everyday "apocalypse" of the millennium (microprocessor) "bug", a transference, perhaps, of the obsession with viral destruction during the last two decades of the twentieth century replacing earlier bacteriological disasters. But for Baudrillard there is something far worse awaiting us: our failure to reach the "end" at all: "... now deterrence has succeeded, we have to get used to the idea that *there is no end any longer, there will no longer be any end*, that history has become interminable" (1994b: 116). Humanity missed the "Big Bang" and now, through the operation of hyperreality, humanity will "miss" the end, experiencing instead a gradual, tedious unfolding of retro history, of simulated returns to events through which a "retrospective absolution" is desired. This endless deferral of the end, through a side-stepping of the real (deterrence, for example, leads to all of our fears being located in the virtual reality of the simulated nuclear war, and then a fading of those fears and a shift in the economic balance of power) leads not to a halting of history, but its "reversal". Baudrillard argues that sometime during the 1980s, "... history took a turn in the opposite direction" (1994b: 10). Theorizing an "apogee of time" (using the spatial metaphor of satellite bodies), a point was reached where linear progression reaches its furthest limits; a gravitational pull then brings time rushing backwards, like a satellite falling back to earth:

> We are faced with a paradoxical process of reversal, a reversive effect of modernity which, having reached its speculative limit and extrapolated all its virtual developments, is disintegrating into its simple elements in a cata-strophic process of recurrence and turbulence.
>
> (1994b: 11)

Thus we try and recover the past reality of war with, for example, the Gulf War, but to no avail: all we have is a war operative and interpreted through the contemporary laws of simulation and the botched attempt to start a "new world order". Baudrillard suggests that behind this desire to return, this reversal of history, is the desire to know where things went wrong, where we slipped imperceptibly into a world of empty simulation: "However, these earlier forms never resurface as they were; they never escape the destiny of extreme modernity. Their resurrection is itself hyper-real" (1994b: 117). In many respects, *The Illusion of the End* becomes Baudrillard's most self-reflexive book; the loss of the symbolic cannot be perceived through nostalgia because then Baudrillard would be attempting a reversal of history, he would not only be complicit in the enterprise, but he would be fooled or seduced by the substitute. But Baudrillard does attempt to find the "points" in time where we slipped from the symbolic to simulation, from the "real" to the sign, and in many respects his entire enterprise can be summarized by the mapping and playful description of this slip-page.

SUMMARY

By comparing Baudrillard's *America* to American postmodernist Don DeLillo's novel *White Noise*, this chapter asserts that one of the problems generated by Baudrillard's work is his refusal to separate fact from fiction. This is marked most strongly in his later writing. The chapter explores this problem with reference to terrorism, simulation and the question of a writing strategy. The latter is explored through the paradoxes and contradictions of Baudrillard's essay "On Nihilism", asking in relation to this: "Who" and "where" is Baudrillard in relation to his own texts? The association with Nietzsche reveals a lot about having different writing strategies or styles, as well as clarifying different types of nihilism. Baudrillard argues that postmodernism is a form of negative nihilism, where the hyperreal is supposed to be "superior" to the real. But Baudrillard's own postmodern writing strategies are at times at odds with his defence of the real – for example, when his writing is experienced like the road movies it mimics in *America*.

AFTER
BAUDRILLARD

Like a meteor entering the Earth's atmosphere, Baudrillard's ideas have broken apart and scattered across a number of critical fields. These include aesthetics, cyberpunk, global media and film theory, new approaches to geography and history, popular culture or cultural studies, and postmodernism. Baudrillard has become part of the postmodern fabric of the contemporary West. In this concluding chapter we will examine some of the ways in which Baudrillard's work has an impact upon these theoretical areas, looking briefly at how other critics have used his work.

ELECTRONIC LANDSCAPES

There is a world developing that breaks away from the old spaces of Fordist industrialization. In other words, the massive production lines situated in large centralized factory spaces are being replaced by decentred and fragmented sites of production. Instead of a large factory being based in one town, in one country, sites of production have become international: it may be cheaper to situate elsewhere, in a number of countries where labour is cheaper and for various reasons more flexible. Not only is the physical site of production fracturing, but the mode of production is changing, too. Thus once heavily industrialized countries are developing new "soft" industries based upon computers, software, leisure industries and the rapid rise of internet technologies. This is a world of virtual reality, with capital flowing rapidly across electronic landscapes, and fortunes being created out of hyperreal companies (such as Internet companies which have no physical product and make no profit, yet are still valued on the stock exchange, regardless of their volatility). Sociologists and geographers are exploring these electronic landscapes and related phenomena using extensively the theories of Jean Baudrillard.

In their book *Spaces of Identity*, David Morley and Kevin Robins state "We believe that what he [Baudrillard] says should be taken very seriously" (1995: 194). Examining "global media, electronic landscapes and cultural boundaries", Morley and Robins explore the post-Fordist world. In this world the human subject is caught in an impossible double-bind between, as Baudrillard points out, the demands of autonomy and submission (1995: 196). In other words, human beings are expected to keep pace with the decentred world with the ability constantly to find new jobs, and in the process re-skill themselves many times (shifting from factory worker perhaps to software writer or financial adviser, and so on). Yet human beings are also expected to be passive consumers, subjected to a mass of advertising, especially television advertising, and whole systems of consumption. Morley and Robins think through this new impossible double-bind in relation to Baudrillard's notions of artificiality and his point that "... the future seems to have shifted towards artificial satellites" (1995: 170). Thus the importance of cybernetics and the ways in which people can become totally immersed, even lost, in virtual reality and other artificial worlds (1995: 169–170). Such cybernetic worlds can be examined in terms of the politics of identity and nationalism that often accompany or even structure them. This latter is being explored today as a kind of "techno-orientalism", where notions of the alien Other are rewritten in terms of cyborgs and cybernetics (Morley and Robins examine the sometimes racist portrayal of the Japanese, for example, as cold technological beings). In more general terms, we now live in a world which often appears dominated by the "global hyperspace" of mass-media corporations such as CNN, News Corporation and Sony. These are virtually stateless enterprises, operating across the world and penetrating homes in almost every country and culture that has access to television and/or newsprint. Again, this world of the television screen and the network is mapped out and theorized at great length by

Baudrillard, and his work is providing critical impetus for new thinkers in this realm.

Paul Rodaway, in a paper called "Exploring the Subject in Hyper-Reality" (1995), examines the contemporary poststructural and postmodernist debates about the subject becoming detached from a contextualized "real" world, just as the sign is now considered to be detached from an original object. He puts Baudrillard into play with a number of leading contemporary thinkers (such as Jacques Derrida and Fredric Jameson), to begin sketching a map of the new "hyper-subject" or "trans-subject". What this means is that the subject is now perceived to be a transitional form, on the road to something or somewhere else. What this might be is yet to be finalized or theorized, but Baudrillard offers a series of critical tools – such as his concept of the hyperreal – with which to articulate the transitional form. Rodaway at times compares Baudrillard's approach with other theorists, to examine the effectiveness of Baudrillard's writing and performing at the limits of thought. Through this comparison emerges the notion that Baudrillard has a radical approach, where the subject has been seduced, fragmented and even destroyed by the dominance of the object. Our technological societies are object-dominated rather than subject-controlled. Rodaway also uses Baudrillard to explore the hyperreal spaces or experiences of contemporary society, especially the reconstructed past in living museums and theme parks.

RETHINKING HISTORY

How useful are Baudrillard's statements on historical revisionism, the notion not that we are at the end of history, but that we are wiping out our own pasts? How useful are Baudrillard's statements for thinkers exploring the intersection of colonial and postcolonial histories, or specific notions of, say, feminist history? Baudrillard's work offers a useful foil for examining contemporary culture and recent history. In many respects Baudrillard is not just some kind of postmodern "prophet" of the future, but a commentator on the present – what is happening in our world, right now. Contemporary historians are examining their subject from a number of new theoretical perspectives. An excellent recent overview of these perspectives can be found in Keith Jenkins' book *Why History? Ethics and Postmodernity* (1995), which includes a challenging short chapter on Baudrillard. Meaghan

Morris, in *Too Soon Too Late* (1998), explores recent Australian history in relation to theoretical models provided by thinkers such as Baudrillard. Her feminist account involves a kind of intellectual combat with Baudrillard, at times finding his concepts such as the hyperreal useful and relevant, and at other times rejecting his work as too located in the theoretical (rather than the contextual) realm of cultural studies. For example, in exploring small-town Australia, Morris analyses the way that the constructions of the past – museums, tourist spaces, simulated historical locations – operate to interpret their own place in or as history. She compares this with Baudrillard's rejection of analogous towns in France in his transference of such questions to America. While Morris questions the validity of Baudrillard's dense theoretical statements, such as America is a "giant hologram", and the application of such statements to precise cultural localities elsewhere, she does find value in the effects of Baudrillard's approach: "... the point about holograms (like simulacra) is that they volatize, rather than replace, other models of signifying practice ..." (1998: 60). The volatility of the juxtaposed "pasts" in small-town Australia is precisely what gives these towns a resistance to universal theory. It is this resistance to universal theories and narratives, this (at times) critical terrorism and extremism, which means that Baudrillard can be utilized to enable the construction of new, indigenous approaches to postcolonial studies, rather than relying on mainly European concepts.

AESTHETICS NOW

One of Baudrillard's attractions is the way he mixes theory with performance, although some critics have argued that this becomes a reduction *of* theory *to* performance. In the realm of aesthetics, Baudrillard has not just been some idle spectator. He has turned his talks into multimedia events around the world, and he invariably attracts large audiences which include non-academics interested in his work. In the mid-1990s Baudrillard travelled to Australia, not just to speak at an academic conference ("Baudrillard in the Nineties: The Art of Theory") but also to attend an exhibition of his own photography at the Institute of Modern Art, Brisbane. Baudrillard's photography is a curious mix of the hyperreal and the authentic, the electronic and the organic; selections can be seen in the collection *Jean Baudrillard: Art and*

Artefact, edited by Nicholas Zurbrugg (1997), alongside some fascinating essays by art theorists, historians and philosophers. This collection makes apparent not only the wide-ranging nature of Baudrillard's comments on aesthetics, but also makes it clear that there are ongoing issues, particularly in the fields of film and photography for future theorists using Baudrillard's work. Critic Timothy Luke summarizes this neatly:

> Jean Baudrillard has exerted unusual influence in the fields of art, aesthetics, and cultural production during the 1980s and 1990s ... Baudrillard's work on simulation, seduction, and hyperreality in the 1980s reverberated strongly among various artist communities, while it also enjoyed an enthusiastic reception in the art criticism network.
>
> (1994: 209)

BAUDRILLARD ONLINE

A good place to start exploring the impact that Baudrillard has had on wide-ranging critical theories, especially the catch-all term "postmodernism" (in that it covers many different ways of writing about, or as, "postmodern"), is the World Wide Web. "Baudrillard on the Web", a site maintained by Alan Taylor at the University of Texas, is a good starting point for any search engine. This site provides many active links to a whole host of material about, or by Baudrillard. One of the quality locations that exist via a hyperlink is the online journal *CTHEORY*, which describes itself as "... an international journal of theory, technology and culture. Articles, interviews, and key book reviews in contemporary discourse are published weekly as well as theorisations of major 'event-scenes' in the mediascape". *CTHEORY* is edited by Arthur and Marilouise Kroker, and contains essays by Baudrillard such as "Disneyworld Company" and "Global Debt and Parallel Universe" (first published in the Parisian newspaper *Libération*). Baudrillard's global debt essay contains interesting comments on the Internet itself, and the ceaseless accumulation of knowledge, being compared to the exponential increase in debt and the countdown to the millennium. This latter relates, finally, to the ways in which Baudrillard has impacted upon so many diverse critical fields. His work continues to have a relevance across many academic domains, even though (or because) it generates a great deal of strong responses from those who reject his approach, especially the later postmodern performances. Baudrillard's work has become part of the very fabric of a postmodern world.

FURTHER READING

WORKS BY JEAN BAUDRILLARD

—— (1968) *Le Système des objets*, Paris: Denoël. (English version, 1997, *The System of Objects*, trans. James Benedict, London & New York: Verso.)

Baudrillard's first book, only fairly recently translated into English. A very clear book, written in a style quite different from the well-known, later "postmodern" pieces. The book uses a structuralist approach that is undoubtedly related to Barthes' *Le Système de la mode* (1964), or "Fashion System". Baudrillard's book is divided into four main sections: "The Functional System", "The Non-Functional System", "The Metafunctional and Dysfunctional System" and "The Socio-Ideological System of Objects and Their Consumption". However, don't let these section titles put you off – the book is a fascinating and enjoyable read, moving from interior design, through "atmosphere", stylization, antiques, collecting, gadgets and robots. *The System of Objects* overall is a new theory of consumption and a description of the relationship between humans and their modern consumer environment.

—— (1970) *La Société de consommation*, Paris: Denoël. (English version, 1998, *The Consumer Society: Myths & Structures*, London: Sage.)

Another one of Baudrillard's early books, only fairly recently translated into English. It is written in a clear style with reference to academic precursors and sources, which is not always the case with the later works. This book is a piece of sociological analysis which continues the project of *The System of Objects*, that is to say it maps out the new consumer world, but in a more theoretical way than the 1968 publication. There are three main sections: "The Formal Liturgy of the Object", "The Theory of Consumption" and "Mass Media, Sex and Leisure". Baudrillard examines the ways in which consumption has gone far beyond the assuaging of needs; instead, consumption is necessary to fuel the system of production. Objects are manipulated now, not simply "consumed"; that is to say, the object is never satisfying, just manipulated alongside every other object, in a never ending process analogous to sign or semiotic systems. Baudrillard also radically re-reads sociologists such as Galbraith, using many examples from American society, which prefigures his own interest in the place for his later postmodern writings. This book is an excellent introduction to the sociological theories that underpin all of Baudrillard's work, and is another highly recommended starting point.

—— (1972) *Pour une critique de l'économie du signe*, Paris: Gallimard. (English version, 1981, *For a Critique of the Political Economy of the Sign*, trans. Charles Levin, US: Telos.)

This book is fundamentally a coherent collection of essays addressing one essential issue in Baudrillard's work: how Marxism needs to be re-read and re-theorized in relation to structuralism and semiotics. Some of these essays or chapters are extremely dense and complicated, such as chapters 6 and 7, "For a General Theory" and "Beyond Use Value". However, this book is still a good place to make sense of the early works of Baudrillard, especially the more readable chapters 5 ("The Art Auction"), 9 ("Requiem for the Media") and 10 ("Design and Environment"). The more complicated chapters are worth reading alongside explanatory material concerning Marxism and semiotics.

—— (1973) *Le Miroir de la production*, Tournail: Casterman. (English version, 1975, *The Mirror of Production*, trans. Mark Poster, St Louis: Telos.)

A book closely related to *For a Critique*, but written in a much more polemical style. In other words, there is less critical "grounding" apparent in this book, and a lot more argument and assertion. Baudrillard's basic premise here is that there has been an overreliance on the Marxist notion of production in contemporary Western thought, and that Marxism needs to be reworked via more complex notions of consumption. There are five main sections in the book: "The Concept of Labor", "Marxist Anthropology and the Domination of Nature", "Historical Materialism and Primitive Societies", "On the Archaic and Feudal Mode" and "Marxism and the System of Political Economy". This is a fairly complex book, at times quite difficult to read because it lacks the clarity and precision of the earlier works. Nonetheless, it marks an important transition in Baudrillard's own thinking.

—— (1976) *L'Échange symbolique et la mort*, Paris: Gallimard. (English version, 1998, *Symbolic Exchange and Death*, trans. Iain Hamilton Grant, London: Sage.)

The first chapter of this book, "The End of Production", continues the argument in *The Mirror of Production*. But the scope of this text is far greater, leading critics such as Mike Gane to write that *Symbolic Exchange and Death* "... is without doubt Jean Baudrillard's most important book" (1991: p.viii). The book has six main sections: "The End of Production", "The Order of Simulacra" (which was translated in the earlier English *Simulations* collection), "Fashion, or the Enchanting Spectacle of the Code", "The Body, or the Mass Grave of Signs", "Political Economy and Death" and "The Extermination of the Name of God". The book overall examines and laments the end of the symbolic and its replacement with the semiotic. We are introduced to the concept of the hyperreal in the chapter on simulacra, and we are given many examples of the way in which everything in modern society operates "semiotically". Many critics consider this to be Baudrillard's last book written in a fairly academic format (with extensive references, and so on, backing up the arguments).

—— (1978) *À l'ombre des majorités silencieuses, ou la fin du social*, Fontenay-sous-Bois: Cahiers d'Utopie. (English version, 1983, *In the Shadow of the Silent Majorities: Or, the End of the Social and Other Essays*, trans. Paul Foss, Paul Patton and John Johnston, New York: Semiotext(e).)

One of Baudrillard's books which appeared in the New York Semiotext(e) series, largely responsible for generating interest and some infamy in the English-speaking world, published as they were before the early French works. The book has four main sections: "In the Shadow of the Silent Majorities", "... Or, the End of the Social", "The Implosion of Meaning in the Media", and "Our Theater of Cruelty". The book examines the notion that "the masses" are not subjected or manipulated, but instead form a "body" impervious to prodding and complex demands. In other words, the masses are more "powerful" than the forces which have traditionally been supposed to direct control. Baudrillard makes a number of radical and contentious statements in this book, including the assertion that the "social" no longer exists and that information "... is directly destructive of meaning and signification" (1978: 96). This short book is an excellent introduction to Baudrillard's "postmodern" writings, both in the sense of content and style of argumentation.

—— (1979) *De la séduction*, Paris: Denoël-Gonthier. (English version, 1990, *Seduction*, trans. B. Singer, London: Macmillan.)

A highly contentious piece of writing from the perspective of feminism, yet one that still initiates debate concerning Baudrillard's "position" in relation to feminist theory. A. Goshorn argues that a critical examination is needed of:

> ... Baudrillard's rather careless employment of the category of "the feminine," particularly in constructing one of his central theoretical figures, the notion of *seduction*. His usage of "the feminine" here and elsewhere in his writing surely appears, on the surface, to be risking a narrowly essentialized definition of the term, and one drawn from the social postures of a previous century at that.
>
> (1979: 258)

Overall, Baudrillard's argument is convoluted and not terribly well presented. A poor text.

—— (1981) *Simulacres et simulation*, Paris:Galilée. (English versions: 1983, part translation, *Simulations*, trans. Paul Foss, Paul Patton and Philip Beitchman, NY: Semiotext(e); 1994, full translation, *Simulacra and Simulation*, trans. Sheila Faria Glaser, Ann Arbor: University of Michigan Press.)

A very important text for any serious study of Baudrillard's relationship to postmodernism. The chapters "The Precession of Simulacra" and "The Implosion of Meaning in the Media" were first made available in the Semiotext(e) translations, but the entire text was not available in English until the excellent translation by Sheila Faria Glaser in 1994. The book overall consists of a number of intensely written yet accessible chapters, covering subjects such as film (e.g. *Apocalypse Now*), the hypermarket and hypercommodity, cloning, holograms and nihilism.

—— (1983) *Les Stratégies fatales*, Paris: Grasset. (English version, 1990, *Fatal Strategies*, trans. Philip Beitchman and W.G.J. Niesluchowski, New York & London: Semiotext(e)/Pluto.)

A performative piece which utilizes a style so annoying to many critics, yet the style is part of the reason that Baudrillard's popularity has remained high amongst a wide range of readers. This book has five main sections: "Ecstasy and Inertia", "Figures of the Transpolitical", "Ironic Strategies", "The Object and Its Destiny" and "For a Principle of Evil". One of the best summaries of the book is written by critic Charles Levin, who writes that: "As an exercise in pure speculation (in the sense of irrational and excessive gambling) it [the book] is also an extraordinary *tour de force*" (1996: 271). Levin argues that for Baudrillard,

> ... the fatal strategy is not a political strategy in the sense of a subject "position" in relation to an object or goal ... The fatal strategy is in a way neither active nor passive, but a kind of magical identification with the actions of things ... one's "opposition" comes out of the system itself.
>
> (1996: 271–272)

—— (1986) *Amérique*, Paris: Grasset. (English version, 1988, *America*, trans. Chris Turner, London & New York: Verso.)

A book which appears to generate equal amounts of support and loathing, praise and ridicule. Essentially a travel narrative or journal broken down into six main sections: "Vanishing Point", "New York", "Astral America", "Utopia Achieved", "The End of US Power?" and "Desert for Ever". Baudrillard deals with, or recycles, a great number of clichés concerning the US, as part of the structural opposition throughout this book between New and Old Worlds (the clichés are initially from the perspective of the Old World, but eventually problematize the New–Old binary opposition). As such, the travel narrative begins to deconstruct the act of writing such a book in the first place; it is therefore postmodern in the sense that it fragments itself or deconstructs itself in the popular use of the latter term. Baudrillard adopts here a contradictory tone of simultaneous insight and naiveté, or he constructs his travel narrative out of the *aporia* or blind spot of this problematic. Overall, the book can be recommended as something very readable and, at the same time, bizarrely impossible to read. Parts of the book are quite dense, if not aphoristic in the Nietzschean sense, and are hard to understand, but if read with the average banal television holiday or travel show in mind, the book can at times be incredibly humorous.

—— (1987) *L'Autre par lui-même*, Paris: Galilée. (English version, 1988, *The Ecstasy of Communication*, trans. Bernard and Caroline Schutze, New York: Semiotext(e).)

The basic premise of this book is fairly simple: that we have moved from the realms of the "scene" to that of the "obscene". The obscene is generated by the transition from spectacle to transparency; according to Baudrillard, the world of the scene and the mirror has given way to the world of the screen and the network (1987a: 12). This book, which is actually a translation of Baudrillard's doctoral dissertation, or *Habilitation*, is available in the hard-hitting Semiotext(e) series. It is composed of six main sections within the usual framework of introduction and conclusion: "The Ecstasy of Communication", "Rituals of Transparency", "Metamorphosis, Metaphor, Metastasis", "Seduction, or, the Superficial Depths", "From the System to the Destiny of Objects" and "Why Theory?" One way of thinking about this book in relation to the earlier sociological and Marxist analyses is with the opening sentence: "... there is no longer a system of objects" (1987a: 11). However, Baudrillard does make the point that his argument in this book is prefigured by Marx's work on the abstractedness of the commodity. Overall, another good point of entry for Baudrillard's writings on postmodernism.

—— (1987) *Cool Memories: 1980–1985*, Paris: Galilée. (English version, 1990, *Cool Memories*, trans. Chris Turner, London & New York: Verso.)

The first of three "journals" by Baudrillard now available. This one covers the years 1980–1984 and a multitude of subjects, most of which are written about with an aphoristic style. Taking two pages at random, there are entries on: the workers, bureaucracy, dreams, theory, love, Hegel, Aristotle and seduction. However, apart from some interesting comments on French poststructuralists, many of the entries are slightly feeble in comparison with much of Baudrillard's work, and certainly do not match the power and interest of Nietzsche's aphorisms.

—— (1991) *La Guerre du golfe n'a pas eu lieu*, Paris: Galilée. (English version, 1995, *The Gulf War Did Not Take Place*, trans. Paul Patton, Sydney: Power.)

A collection of essays brought together to form one small, but highly contentious book. The three sections are: "The Gulf War Will Not Take Place", "The Gulf War: Is It Really Taking Place?" and "The Gulf War Did Not Take Place". The essays originally appeared in *Libération* prior to, during and after the Gulf War. The book analyses the war as a perfect example of hyperreality and is especially good at explaining Baudrillard's notion of "the test", which appears through many of his writings. Paul Patton, in his excellent introduction, notes that Baudrillard is pursuing "... a high risk writing strategy" in this book (1991: 6). It becomes clear that the book illuminates both the problems and the potentialities of Baudrillard's theories and writing strategies. Overall, this is probably one of the best books to start reading and thinking about the "later" Baudrillard, especially because Baudrillard's analyses can be compared to the mass of video and other media material available "on" the Gulf War that he is partly discussing.

—— (1992) *L'Illusion de la fin ou la grève des événements*, Paris: Galilée. (English version, 1994, *The Illusion of the End*, trans. Chris Turner, Cambridge: Polity.)

A collection of essays geared towards the argument that the notion of the millennium/the end of history belongs to a linear, modern concept of history. Instead, Baudrillard argues that we have entered a period whereby history has gone into reverse, through a process of accumulating "effacement". Like many of Baudrillard's "later" writings, essays/chapters are self-contained as well as working as a functional whole, and thus the book can be "dipped into".

—— (1995) *Le Crime parfait*, Paris: Galilée. (English version, 1996, *The Perfect Crime*, trans. Chris Turner, London & New York: Verso.)

The crime here is the "murder of reality", which of course cannot be "perfect" in the sense of being totally complete. Instead, Baudrillard writes because of the fissures still available, enabling him to be aware of the process of the crime. In many ways this book recycles much of the material that figures so prominently in Baudrillard's "later" writings, although there is a slight narrative structure and "feel" to the text that may make it more readable for some. While this book probably doesn't work well at an introductory level, it is an excellent read for those familiar with the bulk of Baudrillard's writings.

WORKS ON JEAN BAUDRILLARD

Butler, Rex (1999) *Jean Baudrillard: The Defence of the Real*, London: Sage.

A very accessible book, with an overview in the introduction and three main sections (Simulation; Seduction; and Doubling). Butler focuses on the sociological aspects of Baudrillard's work.

Gane, Mike (1991) *Baudrillard: Critical and Fatal Theory*, London: Routledge.

Probably the most accessible book on Baudrillard, composed of four main parts (introduction and background; development of Marxism and theoretical positions; analysis of culture, seduction, fatal theory and America; and the double spiral). Gane is exceptionally good at mapping out the Marxist critique of Baudrillard's work.

—— (ed.) (1993) *Baudrillard Live: Selected Interviews* , London & New York: Routledge.

A collection of twenty interviews (given some manipulation of the notion of the interview itself between Baudrillard and Gane), many of which were first published in other locations. This is a valuable resource for the reader of Baudrillard, in terms both of the accessibility to otherwise complex ideas and the range of subjects discussed. A valuable contribution to Baudrillard studies.

Genosko, Gary (1994) *Baudrillard and Signs: Signification Ablaze*, London: Routledge.

An extremely complex book which demands of the reader a reasonably advanced knowledge of structuralist and poststructuralist theory. There are four main sections ("Bar Games", "Simulation and Semiosis", "Varieties of Symbolic Exchange" and "Empty Signs and Extravagant Objects") and an excellent bibliography.

Kellner, Douglas (1989) *Jean Baudrillard: From Marxism to Postmodernism and Beyond*, Cambridge: Polity.

A demanding introduction to Baudrillard that does require a fairly extensive knowledge of background issues, theoretical positions and texts. However, the book does provide a clearly argued critique of Baudrillard, and is probably one of the best places to start in terms of understanding the critical objections to Baudrillard. The book is composed of seven sections ("Commodities", "Needs and Consumption in the Consumer Society", "Beyond Marxism", "Media, Simulation and the End of the Social", "The Postmodern Carnival; Provocations" and "The Metaphysical Imaginary; Beyond Baudrillard").

—— (1994) *Baudrillard: A Critical Reader*, Oxford: Basil Blackwell.
A collection of fourteen critical essays, which vary from "survey"-type approaches to a more critical engagement. Essays cover subjects such as commodification, critical theory and technoculture, semiotics, cybernetics, fashion, media culture, symbolic exchange, hyperreality, simulation, modernism, postmodernism, feminism and cultural politics. There is a clear and useful introduction by Douglas Kellner, which is very critical of Mike Gane's readings of Baudrillard. This is a good place to start thinking not only about the critical issues in Baudrillard's work but also the conflicting interpretations of his work.

Levin, Charles (1996) *Jean Baudrillard: A Study in Cultural Metaphysics*, London: Prentice Hall.
At times complex, this study is broken down into manageable, short sections, which come under seven main headings ("Introduction: Historical and Cultural Context", "Becoming an Object", "Baudrillard in the Politics of Theory", "From History to Metaphysics", "Fatal Strategies", "Metaphysical Ruins and Modernism" and "Postmortemism"). There is an extremely useful glossary of key terms, although the entry on the potlatch is weak.

Pefanis, Julian (1991) *Heterology and the Postmodern: Bataille, Baudrillard, and Lyotard*, Durham and London: Duke University Press.
An excellent, critical account of Baudrillard (see especially chapter 4, "Theories of the Third Order"), which also puts a wide range of contemporary French thinkers into context, showing how they relate to – and critique – one another.

Rojek, Chris and Turner, Bryan S. (eds) (1993) *Forget Baudrillard?*, London & New York: Routledge.

An extensive collection of eight essays, including an excellent analysis and critique of Baudrillard's controversial book *Seduction* by critic Sadie Plant (chapter 5), two essays on *America* and a clear examination of Baudrillard and politics by Chris Rojek (chapter 6).

Zurbrugg, Nicholas (ed.) (1997) *Jean Baudrillard: Art and Artefact*, London: Sage.

A collection of critical essays including three essays and eight colour photographs by Jean Baudrillard and two interviews. The collection is based on a symposium called "Baudrillard in the Nineties: The Art of Theory", held at the Institute of Modern Art, Brisbane, in 1994. There are essays by Baudrillard critics such as Butler, Genosko and Patton, as well as a useful critical bibliography by Richard G. Smith.

WORKS CITED

Ardagh, John (1977) *The New France: A Society in Transition 1945–1977*, London: Penguin.

Bataille, Georges (1985) *Visions of Excess: Selected Writings, 1927–1939*, trans. Allan Stoekl, Carl R. Lovitt and Donald M. Leslie, Jr, Minneapolis: University of Minnesota Press.

Baudrillard, Jean (1975) [1973] *The Mirror of Production*, trans. Mark Poster, St Louis: Telos.

—— (1981) [1972] *For a Critique of the Political Economy of the Sign*, trans. Charles Levin, St Louis: Telos.

—— (1983a) [1978] *In the Shadow of the Silent Majorities: Or, the End of the Social and Other Essays*, trans. Paul Foss, Paul Patton and John Johnston, New York: Semiotext(e).

—— (1983b) [1981] *Simulations*, trans. Paul Foss, Paul Patton and Philip Beitchman, New York: Semiotext(e).

—— (1988a) [1986] *America*, trans. Chris Turner, London & New York: Verso.

—— (1988b) [1987] *The Ecstasy of Communication*, trans. Bernard and Caroline Schutze, New York: Semiotext(e).

—— (1990a) [1987] *Cool Memories*, trans. Chris Turner, London & New York: Verso.

—— (1990b) [1983] *Fatal Strategies*, trans. Philip Beitchman and W.G.J. Niesluchowski, New York & London: Semiotext(e)/Pluto.

—— (1990c) [1979] *Seduction*, trans. B. Singer, London: Macmillan.

—— (1994a) [1981] *Simulacra and Simulation*, trans. Sheila Faria Glaser, Ann Arbor: University of Michigan Press.

—— (1994b) [1992] *The Illusion of the End*, trans. Chris Turner, Cambridge: Polity.

—— (1995) [1991] *The Gulf War Did Not Take Place*, trans. Paul Patton, Sydney: Power.

—— (1996) [1995] *The Perfect Crime*, trans. Chris Turner, London & New York: Verso.

—— (1997) [1968] *The System of Objects*, trans. James Benedict, London & New York: Verso.

—— (1998a) [1976] *Symbolic Exchange and Death*, trans. Iain Hamilton Grant, London: Sage.

—— (1998b) [1970] *The Consumer Society: Myths and Structures*, London: Sage.

Benjamin, Walter (1992) *Illuminations*, trans. Harry Zohn, London: Fontana.

—— (1999) *The Arcades Project*, trans. Howard Eiland and Kevin McLaughlin, Cambridge, MA & London, England: Harvard University Press.

Blackburn, Simon (1996) *Oxford Dictionary of Philosophy*, Oxford: Oxford University Press.

Bracken, Chris (1997) *The Potlatch Papers: A Colonial Case History*, Chicago & London: University of Chicago Press.

Butler, Rex (1999) *Jean Baudrillard: The Defence of the Real*, London: Sage.

Cohen, Robert (ed.) (1998) *Peter Weiss: Marat / Sade, The Investigation, The Shadow of the Body of the Coachman*, New York: Continuum.

Connor, Steven (1989) *Postmodernist Culture: An Introduction to Theories of the Contemporary*, Oxford: Basil Blackwell.

Debord, Guy (1998) *The Society of the Spectacle*, trans. Donald Nicholson-Smith, New York: Zone Books.

Delany, Paul (ed.) (1994) *Vancouver: Representing the Postmodern City*, Vancouver: Arsenal Pulp Press.

Deleuze, Gilles (1983) *Nietzsche and Philosophy*, trans. Hugh Tomlinson, London: Athlone.

DeLillo, Don (1986) [1984] *White Noise*, London: Picador.

—— (1992) *Mao II*, London: Vintage.

Derrida, Jacques (1978) "Structure, Sign and Play in the Discourse of the Human Sciences", in *Writing and Difference*, trans. Alan Bass, Chicago: University of Chicago Press.

Dick, Philip K. (1993) *Do Androids Dream of Electric Sheep (Blade Runner)*, London: HarperCollins.

Emery, Fred (1995) *Watergate: The Corruption and Fall of Richard Nixon*, London: Pimlico.

Eribon, Didier (1991) *Michel Foucault*, trans. Betsy Wing, Cambridge, Massachusetts: Harvard UP.

Ffrench, Patrick (1995) *The Time of Theory: A History of* Tel Quel *(1960–1983)*, Oxford: Clarendon.

Foucault, Michel (1974) *The Order of Things: An Archaeology of the Human Sciences*, London & New York: Tavistock.

—— (1979) *Discipline and Punish: The Birth of the Prison*, trans. Alan Sheridan, New York: Vintage.

Gane, Mike (1991) *Baudrillard: Critical and Fatal Theory*, London: Routledge.

—— (ed.) (1993) *Baudrillard Live: Selected Interviews*, London & New York: Routledge.

Gasché, Rodolphe (1986) *The Tain of the Mirror: Derrida and the Philosophy of Reflection*, Cambridge, MA, & London, England: Harvard University Press.

Genosko, Gary (1994) *Baudrillard and Signs: Signification Ablaze*, London: Routledge.

Gilbert, Helen and Tompkins, Joanne (1996) *Post-Colonial Drama: Theory, Practice, Politics*, London: Routledge.

Hassan, Ihab (1982) *The Dismemberment of Orpheus: Toward a Postmodern Literature*, New York: Oxford University Press.

Hawkes, Terence (1977) *Structuralism and Semiotics*, London: Methuen.

Hegel, Georg Wilhelm Friedrich (1977) *Phenomenology of Spirit*, trans. A.V. Miller, Oxford: Oxford University Press.

Heidegger, Martin (1988) *Hegel's Phenomenology of Spirit*, trans. Parvis Emad and Kenneth Maly, Bloomington & Indianapolis: Indiana University Press.

Hyppolite, Jean (1974) *Genesis and Structure of Hegel's Phenomenology of Spirit*, trans. Samuel Cherniak and John Heckman, Evanston: Northwestern University Press.

Jameson, Fredric (1998) *The Cultural Turn: Selected Writings on the Postmodern, 1938–1998*, London & New York: Verso.

Jencks, Charles (1987) *The Language of Post-Modern Architecture*, London: Academy Editions.

Jenkins, Keith (1999) *Why History? Ethics and Postmodernity*, London & New York: Routledge.

Kellner, Douglas (1989) *Jean Baudrillard: From Marxism to Postmodernism and Beyond*, Cambridge: Polity.

—— (1994) *Baudrillard: A Critical Reader*, Oxford: Basil Blackwell.

Kojève, Alexandre (1969) *Introduction to the Reading of Hegel*, trans. J.H. Nicholas, New York: Basic.

Lane, Richard (1993) "The Double Guide: Through the Labyrinth with Robert Kroetsch", *Journal of Commonwealth Literature* 29(2): 19–27.

—— (1999) "Fractures: Written Displacements in Canadian/US Literary Relations", in Deborah Madsen (ed.) *Post-Colonial Literatures: Expanding the Canon*, London: Pluto.

Larkin, Maurice (1991) *France Since the Popular Front: Government and People 1936–1986*, Oxford: Clarendon.

Lefebvre, Henri (1991) *Critique of Everyday Life*, trans. John Moore, London: Verso.

Levin, Charles (1996) *Jean Baudrillard: A Study in Cultural Metaphysics*, London: Prentice Hall.

Luke, Timothy W. (1994) "Aesthetic Production and Cultural Politics: Baudrillard and Contemporary Art", in Douglas Kellner (ed.) *Baudrillard: A Critical Reader*, Oxford: Blackwell.

Lyotard, Jean-François (1984) *The Postmodern Condition: A Report on Knowledge*, trans. Geoff Bennington and Brian Massumi, Minneapolis: University of Minnesota Press.

Marx, Karl (1979) *Capital: A Critique of Political Economy*, vol. 1, trans. Ben Fowkes, Harmondsworth: Penguin.

Mauss, Marcel (1990) *The Gift: The Form and Reason for Exchange in Archaic Societies*, London & New York: Routledge.

Morley, David and Robins, Kevin (1995) *Spaces of Identity: Global Media, Electronic Landscapes and Cultural Boundaries*, London & New York: Routledge.

Morris, Meaghan (1998) *Too Soon Too Late: History in Popular Culture*, Bloomington & Indianapolis: Indiana University Press.

Nehamas, Alexander (1985) *Nietzsche: Life as Literature*, Cambridge, MA & London: Harvard University Press.

Norris, Christopher (1992) *Postmodernism, Intellectuals and the Gulf War*, London: Lawrence and Wishart.

Pefanis, Julian (1991) *Heterology and the Postmodern: Bataille, Baudrillard, and Lyotard*, Durham, NC and London: Duke University Press.

Pile, Steve and Thrift, Nigel. (eds) (1995) *Mapping the Subject: Geographies of Cultural Transformation*, London & New York: Routledge.

Rodaway, Paul (1995) "Exploring the Subject in Hyper-Reality", in Steve Pile and Nigel Thrift (eds) *Mapping the Subject: Geographies of Cultural Transformation*, London & New York: Routledge, pp. 241–266.

Rojek, Chris and Turner, Bryan S. (eds) (1993) *Forget Baudrillard?*, London & New York: Routledge.

Spengler, Oswald (1926) *The Decline of the West*, vols. 1 and 2, London: George Allen and Unwin.

Taylor, Charles (1989) *Hegel*, Cambridge: Cambridge University Press.

Weiss, Peter (1971) *Discourse on Vietnam*, trans. Geoffrey Skelton, London: Calder & Boyers.

Wittgenstein, Ludwig (1993) *Philosophical Occasions: 1912–1951*, Indianapolis & Cambridge: Hackett.

Zurbrugg, Nicholas (ed.) (1997) *Jean Baudrillard: Art and Artefact*, London: Sage.

INDEX